Management Accounting: Budgeting

Tutorial

Aubrey Penning

Published by Osborne Books Limited
Tel 01905 748071
Email books@osbornebooks.co.uk
Website www.osbornebooks.co.uk

Design by Laura Ingham

Printed by CPI Group (UK) Limited, Croydon, CR0 4YY, on environmentally friendly, acid-free paper from managed forests.

British Library Cataloguing in Publication Data
A catalogue record for this book is available from the British Library

ISBN 978 1909173 897

Contents

Introduction

Qualifications covered

This book has been written specifically to cover the Unit 'Management Accounting: Budgeting' which is mandatory for the following qualifications:

AAT Professional Diploma in Accounting – Level 4

AAT Professional Diploma in Accounting at SCQF Level 8

Certificate: Accounting (Level 5 AATSA)

The book contains a clear text with worked examples and case studies, chapter summaries and key terms to help with revision. Each chapter concludes with a wide range of activities, many in the style of AAT computer based assessments.

Osborne Study and Revision Materials

The materials featured on the previous page are tailored to the needs of students studying this Unit and revising for the assessment. They include:

- **Workbooks:** paperback books with practice activities and exams
- **Student Zone:** access to Osborne Books online resources
- **Osborne Books App:** Osborne Books ebooks for mobiles and tablets

Visit www.osbornebooks.co.uk for details of study and revision resources and access to online material.

1 Management accounting techniques

this chapter covers...

In this chapter we examine some of the management accounting techniques that underpin the use of budgets. Most of these techniques will be familiar to you from your earlier studies, while others may be introduced here for the first time.

We start with a reminder of the differences between financial accounting and management accounting (of which budgeting is an important part). We then review the three main methods of costing – absorption costing, marginal costing, and activity based costing (ABC – which is a more sophisticated development of absorption costing).

The next section explains how the costing system used can influence reported profit due to the overhead that may be absorbed into inventory valuations. This has the effect of moving costs between periods when inventory levels change.

The following section deals with cost behaviour and reinforces your earlier studies, including use of the high-low method for analysing semi-variable costs.

The chapter concludes with a section on how the functional structure of an organisation is used in conjunction with budgeting and reporting.

INTRODUCTION TO BUDGETING

In this book we are going to learn about the purposes of budgeting, and how to prepare and use budgets. Budgeting is part of management accounting, and deals with the preparation and use of financial plans for an organisation.

In order to do this we need to understand how budgets fit in with other management accounting systems and techniques. In this first chapter we will review the accounting environment that budgeting operates in, and learn some techniques that we will then apply to budgets later in the book.

FINANCIAL ACCOUNTING AND MANAGEMENT ACCOUNTING

financial accounting

Financial accounting is concerned with recording accounting information so that accounts can be published and used by those outside the organisation. It is governed by legislation and accounting standards, and focuses on the needs of stakeholders from outside the organisation, like shareholders, creditors, and prospective investors. Strict formats and timescales are imposed on organisations that determine exactly how and when the information is produced.

management accounting

Management accounting is the general term used for the production of accounting information for those inside an organisation. Because it is an internal system there are no external rules about how or when the information should be produced. Management accounting exists to help managers plan, monitor, control, and make decisions about the organisation. Its emphasis is on providing information that can help with the future of the organisation. The guiding principle for management accounting information is that it should be **useful** to its readers. If the information fails that simple test, then it has been a pointless waste of time producing it! Budgeting is part of management accounting.

financial and management accounting compared

The table on the next page sets out a summary of the main differences between financial accounting and management accounting.

financial and management accounting compared		
	Financial Accounting	**Management Accounting**
Users	• External Stakeholders	• Internal
Format	• Summarised	• Specific
Governed by	• Legislation & Standards	• Usefulness
Frequency of Information	• Annual (& possible six monthly)	• As required
Time Focus	• Past	• Present and Future

If you look at the diagram below you will see that the activities on the left-hand side relate to 'Financial Accounting', while those on the right-hand side relate to 'Management Accounting'.

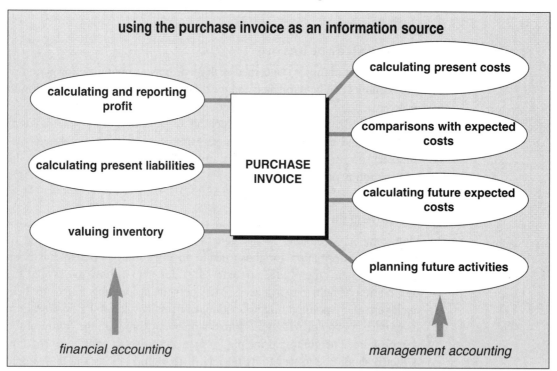

MANAGEMENT ACCOUNTING SYSTEMS

Budgeting is used in organisations that have established management accounting and costing systems, and will integrate with the systems. This is so that the budgets are produced using the same methods as the accounts.

It is therefore important that you fully understand the main management accounting systems, especially the contrasting ways that overhead (indirect) costs can be dealt with. Over the next few pages we will review the systems of absorption costing, marginal costing, and activity based costing.

methods of costing

Management accounting is the branch of accounting that deals with providing internal information within an organisation. Providing costing information is an important area of management accounting, and you will be familiar with the principles of costing from your earlier studies. Just as management accounting has no external rules governing how it should be carried out, cost information can also be developed in various ways. Although costing systems should always be tailored to the needs of the organisation and its managers, there are three general approaches to costing that you will need to become familiar with. They all attempt to calculate a cost for the units that the organisation produces. These 'units of output' could be bicycle wheels made by a bicycle component manufacturer, or operations carried out in a hospital.

- **Absorption Costing**

  This is a system that attempts to determine a 'full' cost for each unit of output. It therefore includes both direct and indirect costs, and uses the mechanisms of allocation, apportionment and absorption to incorporate the indirect costs.

- **Marginal Costing**

  This costing system categorises costs according to their cost behaviour, and divides them simply into variable and fixed costs. This system uses a cost for each unit of output based purely on the variable (or 'marginal') costs. All fixed costs are regarded as time based and are therefore linked to accounting periods rather than units of output.

- **Activity Based Costing (ABC)**

  This is a development of absorption costing, and uses a more sophisticated system to deal mainly with the indirect costs. This involves examining the costs to determine what causes them, and using this information to charge the costs to the units of output in an appropriate manner.

  You will need to understand the workings and implications of these three systems, so we will now examine each one in more detail.

ABSORPTION COSTING

You will probably be familiar with the absorption costing process from your earlier studies, but the following will enable you to recall firstly the terminology and then the steps involved.

terminology

■ **Direct Costs**

Costs that are directly attributable to the units of output. They can be divided into Direct Materials, Direct Labour, and Direct Expenses.

■ **Indirect Costs**

Costs that cannot be directly attributed to the units of production. They are also referred to as overheads. In a manufacturing environment only the indirect costs relating to production are usually absorbed into the product cost.

■ **Cost Centres**

Parts of the organisation where it is convenient to gather costs. It could be a department or section, or an area where a certain activity is carried out. 'Production' cost centres are where the unit of output has some activity carried out on it, whereas 'Service' cost centres provide a service to other cost centres rather than do anything directly to the units of output.

■ **Absorption Bases**

The methods available to absorb cost from the production cost centres into the units of output (or products). All absorption bases use expected (or budgeted) costs and activity levels to work out an absorption rate. Examples of absorption bases are Direct Labour Hours, Machine Hours, and Units of Output.

steps in absorption costing

1 Costs are divided into direct costs and indirect costs. The direct costs can immediately form part of the cost of the units of output, while the indirect costs (overheads) will need to be absorbed into the cost of the units via the next stages.

2 Indirect costs are either allocated to one cost centre (if the cost relates to only one cost centre), or apportioned to several cost centres by some fair system (if the cost relates to several cost centres). For example, rent costs might be apportioned using the area of the building used by each cost centre.

3   If costs have now accumulated into service cost centres, the total cost of each service cost centre is shared amongst the production cost centres that benefit from the service provided. This is carried out using secondary apportionment. For example the total cost of running the stores service cost centre could be shared out by using the numbers of requisitions from the various production cost centres as a basis for secondary apportionment.

4   The costs that have been gathered in the production cost centres can now be absorbed into the units of output by using a predetermined absorption rate based on the expected activity level. The indirect cost is absorbed from the cost centre into the units of output as they pass through the cost centre. A common basis for this absorption is direct labour hours, so that the longer a product is worked on in the production cost centre, the greater the amount of cost is absorbed. An absorption rate is also known as an **overhead recovery rate**.

Case Study

THE ABSORPTION COMPANY: ABSORPTION COSTING

The Absorption Company manufactures several products, one of which is the Sorp. Its factory is divided into two production cost centres (Assembly and Finishing) and one service cost centre (Maintenance). 80% of the activity in the Maintenance cost centre benefits Assembly, while the remainder benefits Finishing.

Before the financial period started the expected indirect costs for the forthcoming year were:

	£
Assembly	208,000
Finishing	72,000
Maintenance	40,000

Each unit of Sorp uses direct material that costs £42. It takes five direct labour hours in Assembly and two direct labour hours in Finishing to make one unit of Sorp. Indirect costs are absorbed from the production cost centres using a direct labour hour rate. The expected direct labour hours for the year were 120,000 in Assembly and 25,000 in Finishing. All direct labour hours are paid at £8.00.

required

Calculate the following:

1   The indirect cost absorption rate in each of the two production cost centres.

2   The absorbed cost of one unit of Sorp.

solution

1 the indirect absorption rate

	Assembly	Finishing	Maintenance
Expected Indirect Costs:	£	£	£
Allocated / Apportioned	208,000	72,000	40,000
Secondary Apportionment	32,000	8,000	(40,000)
Total	240,000	80,000	
Expected Direct Labour Hours	120,000	25,000	

Absorption Rates:
Assembly   £240,000 ÷ 120,000   = £2.00 per direct labour hour
Finishing   £80,000 ÷ 25,000   = £3.20 per direct labour hour

2 the absorbed cost of one Sorp

		Cost of one unit of Sorp:
Direct Materials		£42.00
Direct Labour:		
Assembly 5 hours @ £8.00	£40.00	
Finishing 2 hours @ £8.00	£16.00	
		£56.00
Indirect Costs:		
Assembly 5 hours @ £2.00	£10.00	
Finishing 2 hours @ £3.20	£6.40	
		£16.40
Total Absorbed Cost		£114.40

MARGINAL COSTING

Marginal costing accepts that there is a fundamental difference between costs that are based, not on the origin of the costs, but purely on the behaviour of the costs when the activity level (or output level) changes. There are four main ways that the costs could behave within a range of activity levels:

Variable Costs   Costs where the total amount varies in proportion to the activity level when the activity level changes. Variable costs are also known as marginal costs when using marginal costing.

Fixed Costs   Costs that do not change when the level of activity changes (within certain parameters).

Step Costs   Costs that change in steps at certain levels of activity, remaining unchanged (fixed) in-between.

| **Semi-variable Costs** | Costs where a part of the cost acts as a variable cost, and a part acts as a fixed cost. |

All the costs (regardless of whether they might be viewed as direct or indirect) need to be divided into variable costs and fixed costs. Semi-variable costs are divided into their fixed and variable components. There are numerical techniques for dividing them into variable and fixed elements. One of these, the 'high-low' method, is reviewed later in this chapter. Once the total variable and fixed costs have been determined, only the variable (or marginal) costs are linked to the units of output to provide a cost per unit. This enables a 'contribution' towards the fixed costs (and ultimately profit) to be calculated either per unit, or for a specified output level.

| **Unit Contribution** | The difference between the selling price per unit and the variable costs per unit. It is the amount that each unit sold contributes towards the fixed costs of the organisation and profit. |
| **Total Contribution** | The difference between the sales income and the variable costs of the units sold in a period. This amount is the total contribution that the sales of all the units in the period make towards the fixed costs of the organisation and profit. |

Fixed costs are taken straight to the profit statement, and are deducted from the total contribution for the period to arrive at the profit for the period. You will need to be familiar with marginal costing, and recognise and use the formats and terminology that apply to this system.

Marginal costing has considerable advantages over absorption costing when it is used to help with making decisions. Uses of marginal costing are also explored in the unit 'Management Accounting: Decision and Control'.

Case Study

THE MARGINAL COMPANY: MARGINAL COSTING

The Marginal Company manufactures one product, the Marg. The following costs relate to a financial year, when 100,000 units of Marg are made:

Direct Materials	£350,000
Direct Labour	£230,000
Indirect Costs	£310,000

Investigations into the behaviour of the costs have revealed the following information:

- Direct Materials behave as variable costs.
- Direct Labour behaves as a variable cost.
- Of the Indirect Costs, £270,000 behaves as a fixed cost, and the remainder as a variable cost.

required

1 Calculate the cost of one unit of Marg using Marginal Costing.

2 If each unit of Marg sells for £10, and all the production of 100,000 units is sold, draft a marginal costing statement for the financial year showing the contribution (per unit and in total), and the profit for the year.

solution

1 costing a unit of Marg

Using only the variable (marginal) costs to cost one unit of Marg:

Direct Materials (£350,000 ÷ 100,000)	£3.50
Direct Labour (£230,000 ÷ 100,000)	£2.30
Variable Overheads	
(£310,000 − £270,000 = £40,000) ÷ 100,000	£0.40
Total marginal cost per unit	£6.20

2 Marginal Costing Statement for the Financial Year

	Per Unit £	For Year £
Sales	10.00	1,000,000
Less Variable Costs	6.20	620,000
Contribution	3.80	380,000
Less Fixed Overheads		270,000
Profit		110,000

Note that the fixed costs are not calculated in per unit terms, but are simply deducted in total from the total contribution.

ACTIVITY BASED COSTING (ABC)

background to ABC

Activity based costing was developed in the 1970s and 1980s as an alternative to absorption costing. Since the time when absorption costing was initially developed (at the time of the Industrial Revolution), many aspects of manufacture had changed, and it was felt that absorption costing was not providing information of sufficient quality. The points that were made by advocates of ABC were:

Overheads (indirect costs) typically now account for the major part of product costs, and should therefore be accounted for in a less arbitrary way than they would under absorption costing. For example, simply absorbing based on just one basis (eg direct labour hours) does not acknowledge the complexity of costs that can make up overheads.

Both production methods and batch sizes can have a major impact on product costs, yet these are largely ignored by absorption costing. For example, the cost involved in setting up equipment will be far greater per unit of output for small production runs than for large ones.

Modern production methods do not lend themselves to the use of absorption rates such as direct labour hours or machine hours. Integrated production systems can often operate with minimal human intervention.

cost pools and cost drivers

ABC works by identifying the indirect activities, and grouping their costs into 'cost pools', one for each major activity. For each cost pool there must be a factor that drives the costs and causes those costs to change. This 'cost driver' is identified and its rate calculated. The rate is then used to charge the output with cost, based on the output's use of the activity.

For example, in a stores department (which would typically form one service cost centre under absorption costing), the activities could be determined as:

1   Receiving goods inwards, and

2   Issuing goods to production.

The costs of running the stores department would be analysed into the costs for carrying out each of these activities – the 'cost pools'. The cost drivers might be agreed as:

1   Number of Deliveries Received (for receiving goods inward), and

2   Number of Requisitions (for issuing goods).

The rate per cost driver would then be calculated by dividing the cost pool by the cost driver for that pool.

Using this technique, a product that required many different components that were delivered separately and then issued frequently to production, would be charged with a high cost from the activities in the stores department. In comparison a product that was made from components delivered together and issued to production in bulk would incur fewer costs.

Using a suitable analysis of costs and their drivers an organisation can adapt the system to its own circumstances. Each different product will then be charged with a more accurate cost based on its use of the activities than if absorption costing had been used.

The diagram on the next page shows how the system works. Study it and then read the two Case Studies that follow. They both illustrate the application of activity based costing, the first in a manufacturing company and the second to a college operating in the service sector.

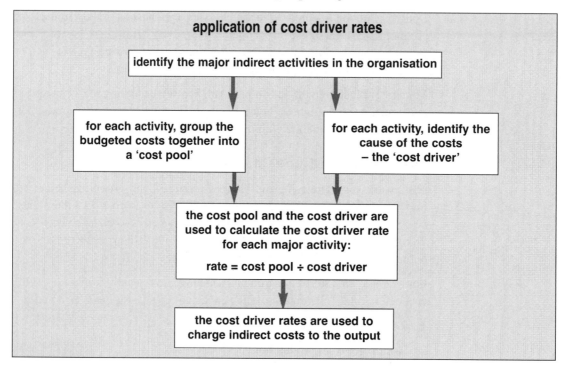

ABC COMPANY: ACTIVITY BASED COSTING

Case Study

The ABC Company has introduced activity based costing to cost its output. It makes several products on mechanised production lines, including AB, and BC. AB is a product that is usually made in large batches of 1,000 units, since it sells in large quantities. BC is a specialised product selling to a niche market, and is therefore made in small batches of 20 units.

As a part of the introduction of ABC the company has identified one major activity as 'setting up the production equipment'. The cost associated with this activity in a financial year is budgeted at £250,000, and therefore this amount forms the cost pool for setting up production equipment.

The company has identified the cost driver of this activity as 'number of set-ups performed', since if the number increases the cost will be proportionally greater. One batch of any product requires one set-up to be performed.

The budgeted figure of £250,000 was based on an estimated 500 set-ups in the financial year.

The unit costs for AB and BC have already been calculated excluding the set-up costs, as follows:

AB	£50.00 per unit
BC	£55.00 per unit

required

Calculate the total cost per unit of AB and BC, including set-up costs.

solution

The cost driver rate for set-ups = £250,000 ÷ 500 = £500 per set up

Charging at this rate:

One unit of AB would incur set-up cost of £500 ÷ 1,000 = £0.50

One unit of BC would incur set-up cost of £500 ÷ 20 = £25.00

Incorporating this into the previous costs gives per unit costs of:

	AB	BC
	£	£
Costs excluding set-ups	50.00	55.00
Cost of set-ups	0.50	25.00
Total Cost	50.50	80.00

In this Case Study set-ups account for approximately 1% of the total cost of a unit of AB, compared to 31% of the total cost of a unit of BC. These differences would not be identified using a traditional absorption costing system that treated set-ups as a part of general overheads.

Case Study

AB COLLEGE:
ACTIVITY BASED COSTING IN THE SERVICE SECTOR

The Activity Based College is a small private college, providing a variety of part-time business related courses. The college has determined that there are four major activities that are undertaken, that have the following cost pools for the financial year and cost drivers.

Activity	Cost Pool	Cost Driver Information
Teaching	£500,000	Teaching Hours (25,000 in year)
Course Preparation	£300,000	New Courses (30 in year)
Lesson Preparation	£100,000	Teaching Hours (25,000 in year)
Student Administration	£100,000	Number of Students (1,000 in year)

The costs for two separate courses are to be calculated using ABC.

The first is the Advanced Marketing Course. This course will run for 250 teaching hours, and should attract 20 students. The course has been run previously.

The second is a new course in Taxation for Exporters to Scandinavia. The course will run for 100 teaching hours, and there are five prospective students.

required

Calculate the cost per course and cost per student for each of the two courses.

solution

First the cost driver rates need to be established:

Teaching	£500,000 ÷ 25,000	= £20 per teaching hour
Course Preparation	£300,000 ÷ 30	= £10,000 per new course
Lesson Preparation	£100,000 ÷ 25,000	= £4 per teaching hour
Student Administration	£100,000 ÷ 1,000	= £100 per student

Secondly these rates are applied to the courses according to their demand for the activities:

1 Advanced Marketing Course

Teaching	£20 x 250 =	£5,000
Course Preparation	(existing course)	-
Lesson Preparation	£4 x 250 =	£1,000
Student Administration	£100 x 20 =	£2,000
Cost for course		£8,000
Cost per student	£8,000 ÷ 20 =	£400

2 Taxation for Exporters to Scandinavia

Teaching	£20 x 100 =	£2,000
Course Preparation	£10,000 x 1 =	£10,000
Lesson Preparation	£4 x 100 =	£400
Student Administration	£100 x 5 =	£500
Cost for course		£12,900
Cost per student	£12,900 ÷ 5 =	£2,580

COSTING SYSTEMS AND RECORDED PROFIT

variations in inventory (stock) valuation

One of the reasons that organisations use a costing system is so that the value of the inventory of finished goods (and work in progress) can be calculated and incorporated into profit statements. Since the different approaches to costing that we have examined give different costs per unit, they will result in different valuations of inventory, this will in turn affect the profit calculation when inventory levels change. A marginal costing system will value inventory at just the variable costs, but a system that absorbs fixed costs into the inventory valuation can result in fixed costs being charged to a period other than the one in which they were incurred.

the effect of inventory valuation on profit

The costs incurred in producing goods in a period, together with the cost of the opening inventory must equal the cost of sales for the period, added to the cost of the closing inventory.

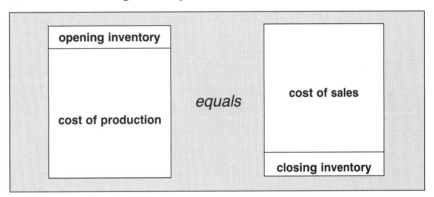

The valuation of the closing inventory will therefore affect the cost of sales and therefore recorded profit.

The following Case Study uses the same data under different costing systems to illustrate the situation.

Case Study

THE ALTERNATIVE COMPANY: COSTING METHODS AND PROFIT

The Alternative Company manufactures a single product, and produces monthly management accounts.

In each of Month 1 and Month 2, 10,000 units were produced, and the following costs were incurred:

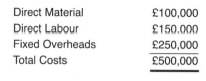

Direct Material	£100,000
Direct Labour	£150,000
Fixed Overheads	£250,000
Total Costs	£500,000

Both the costs and the volume of output were in line with the budget.

Units were sold for £70 each, and in Month 1 the whole production of 10,000 units were sold, whereas in Month 2 only 8,000 units were sold. There was no inventory at the start of Month 1.

Direct Material and Direct Labour are both variable costs.

required

1 Calculate the cost per unit using:
   (a) absorption costing using units as an absorption base
   (b) marginal costing

2 Draft management accounts for each month using:
   (a) absorption costing
   (b) marginal costing

3 Comment on the reasons for any difference in profits.

solution

1 Calculation of cost per unit

(a)   Absorption Costing (using all costs)

   £500,000 ÷ 10,000 = £50 per unit

(b)   Marginal Costing (using variable costs only)

   £250,000 ÷ 10,000 = £25 per unit

2 Producing management accounts

(a)   **Absorption Costing**

		Month 1		Month 2
Sales		£700,000		£560,000
Less cost of sales:				
Opening inventory	–		–	
Cost of production				
(10,000 x £50)	£500,000		£500,000	
Less closing inventory	–			
(2,000 x £50)			£100,000	
		£500,000		£400,000
Profit		£200,000		£160,000

(b)   **Marginal Costing**

	Month 1	Month 2
Sales	£700,000	£560,000
Less variable cost of sales:		
Opening inventory	–	–
Variable cost of production		
(10,000 x £25)	£250,000	£250,000
Less closing inventory	–	
(2,000 x £25)		£50,000
	£250,000	£200,000
Contribution	£450,000	£360,000
Less fixed costs	£250,000	£250,000
Profit	£200,000	£110,000

3 Comments on the reasons for differences in profit

The profits are identical when there is no change in inventory level, as in Month 1, when both opening and closing inventories are zero. However when the inventory level changes between the start and end of the period (as in Month 2) the inventory valuation has an impact on profit.

The additional reported profit of £50,000 (£160,000 compared with £110,000) by using the absorption system is due to £50,000 of the fixed costs being absorbed into the closing inventory and effectively carried into the next period. If the inventory again fell to nil in Month 3 the profit difference would be reversed.

The differences in reported profits are only timing differences – the differences in profit are just reported in different periods.

conclusion

- Where inventory levels increase, absorption costing will record a higher profit than marginal costing, as more of the cost incurred is pushed into the next period.
- Where inventory levels decrease, absorption costing will record a lower profit than marginal costing, as more of the costs from the previous period are set against income.
- Where inventory levels are constant, then, providing there has been no change in unit costs, there will be no difference in recorded profit under either system.

You can therefore see that if an organisation uses absorption costing, significantly building up (or reducing) inventory levels can distort profits.

COST BEHAVIOUR

Earlier in this chapter we noted that marginal costing relies on cost behaviour to divide costs between fixed and variable costs. We will now examine cost behaviour in a little more detail, ready to apply our knowledge and skills to budgets later in the book.

The main types of cost behaviour which you need to understand are:

■ variable costs

■ fixed costs

■ step costs

■ semi-variable costs

variable costs

A cost is described as variable if the total cost varies in direct proportion to the level of activity. In other words, it depends on the number of cost units, the amount per unit being constant.

Total variable cost = variable cost per unit x number of units

For example:

Quenchit Ltd is a water bottling company. The cost to the company of the bottles used is £0.08 each. The total cost of bottles varies in proportion to the number of bottles used and is therefore a variable cost.

Total cost of bottles = £0.08 x number of bottles used.

A graph showing the behaviour of the total cost against level of activity is shown below.

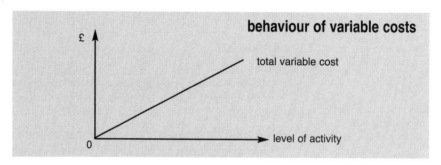

In some cases, the cost per unit may remain constant only within a certain relevant range of levels of activity. Large changes in the number of units produced may alter the cost per unit and hence the behaviour of the total cost. For example, the cost per unit of direct materials may be reduced by bulk purchase discounts when larger amounts are required.

Case Study

KANN LIMITED:
VARIABLE COSTS

Kann Ltd manufactures metal boxes. The total cost of direct materials is £42,000 for making 350,000 boxes and £51,600 for making 430,000 boxes.

required

1 Calculate Kann Ltd's direct material cost per unit at each of the given levels of output and hence determine whether it behaves as a variable cost.

2 Calculate the total cost of direct materials for making 400,000 boxes.

solution

1 £42,000 for 350,000 boxes: £42,000 ÷ 350,000 = £0.12 per box

£51,600 for 430,000 boxes: £51,600 ÷ 430,000 = £0.12 per box

Therefore direct material cost is a constant amount per unit and hence behaves as a variable cost. We can assume it is £0.12 per box for output between 350,000 boxes and 430,000 boxes.

2 Output of 400,000 boxes is within this range.

Total variable cost = variable cost per unit x number of units

For 400,000 boxes:

Total direct material cost = £0.12 x 400,000 = £48,000.

fixed costs

A cost is described as fixed if the total cost does not change when the level of activity changes.

The fixed nature of the cost will only apply when the level of activity changes within a certain relevant range. If major changes occur, such as doubling production or ceasing to make a product, then most costs are likely to change.

Rent is an example of a fixed cost, because once rent is paid to have space available, changes in the amount of work carried out in that space will not affect the total rent. The relevant range would cover the amounts of work possible within the space available. The rent would change if the amount of work increased beyond this capacity.

Notice that in defining fixed costs, we are not referring to costs remaining unchanged from one time period to another. All costs will eventually change over periods of time. A graph showing the behaviour of the total cost against level of activity for a fixed cost is shown below.

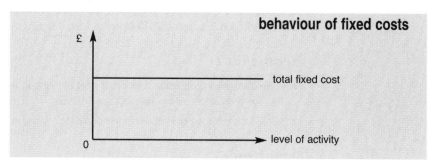

step costs (or stepped-fixed costs)

A cost is described as a step cost if its total changes in steps at certain levels of activity, remaining unchanged in-between.

The name clearly corresponds to the graph showing the behaviour of the total cost against level of activity for a step cost – see below.

Costs which behave as step costs are often related to machines or people who can deal with any number of units of work, up to a maximum number. When the maximum is reached, an additional machine or person is required.

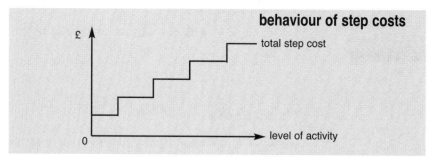

examples

A **pre-school nursery** requires one carer for every six children. For more than six and up to twelve children, two carers are required. For thirteen, another carer must be employed, and so on. The total cost of carers' wages will behave as a step cost.

The **reprographics department** of a large organisation uses photocopiers which are leased. Each machine can produce 10,000 copies in a given period. If the organisation's requirements go above 10,000 for the period, another machine will be leased. The total cost of leasing photocopiers will behave as a step cost.

semi-variable costs

A cost is described as semi-variable (or sometimes semi-fixed) if the total cost is made up of a variable part and a fixed part.

Any cost which consists of a fixed charge plus an amount per unit is a semi-variable cost. Telephone bills may be of this form: a fixed line rental plus a variable amount dependent on the number of minutes of call time, for example.

Total semi-variable cost = Fixed cost + (variable cost per unit x number of units)

The graph showing the behaviour of the total cost against level of activity for a semi-variable cost is shown below. The calculation is illustrated in the Case Study on the next page.

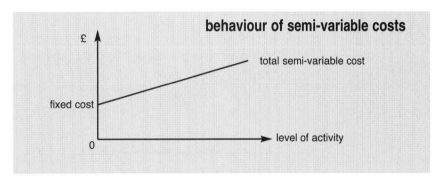

limitations of cost behaviour analysis

The four kinds of cost behaviour described above are not the only possible cost behaviour patterns. In some cases, the actual behaviour of the cost may only approximate to one of these patterns, but useful information can still be obtained using the approximation. Also, a particular pattern of behaviour may only be applicable within a certain relevant range of levels of activity, but again useful information can be obtained within that range.

Using a pattern of behaviour to calculate costs for a level of activity within a given range is called 'interpolation'. Calculations for levels outside the range involve 'extrapolation' and careful consideration must be given to the usefulness of the information obtained in this case, because it may not be realistic to assume that the pattern of behaviour will continue beyond the given range.

The assumption underlying marginal costing is that all costs behave as fixed, variable or semi-variable costs, so that the total of all costs of an organisation can be split into fixed and variable parts. Provided that this assumption is realistic over a relevant range of levels of activity, then useful information can be obtained.

MILLIE LIMITED:
SEMI-VARIABLE COSTS

Production overheads in a manufacturing company have been identified as semi-variable. They consist of fixed costs of £120,000 plus £2.80 per unit produced, for a range of levels of production from 15,000 units to 30,000 units for the period.

required

Calculate the total production overheads for:

1   20,000 units

2   24,500 units

Why would the same calculation be inappropriate for 40,000 units?

solution

1   Total production overheads for 20,000 units would be:

   £120,000 + (£2.80 x 20,000)

   =   £120,000 + £56,000

   =   £176,000

2   Total production overheads for 24,500 units would be:

   £120,000 + (£2.80 x 24,500)

   = £120,000 + £68,600

   = £188,600

The part of the calculation in brackets is the variable part of the cost, which depends on the number of units.

It would not be realistic to use this data and this method to calculate the total production overheads for 40,000 units, because that level of activity is beyond the relevant range. We cannot assume the same cost behaviour exists outside the relevant range.

The following graph illustrates the behaviour of the total cost in this Case Study.

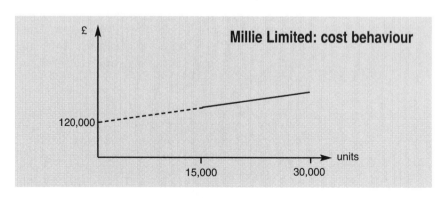

the high-low method

It is important to be able to split a semi-variable cost into its fixed and variable parts. The fixed part will remain unchanged and the variable part can be calculated for a different level of activity. The method you will be expected to use to analyse a semi-variable cost is the 'high-low' method or 'incremental approach', which may be familiar to you from your earlier studies.

The high-low method can be used where the total of a semi-variable cost is known for at least two different activity levels. If the total is known for more than two levels, then the highest and lowest are chosen for the calculation.

The Case Study that follows illustrates the high-low method.

Case Study

HILO PRODUCTS:
THE HIGH-LOW METHOD

Hilo Products makes ladders. We are given the total of a semi-variable cost at four different levels of activity, as follows:

Level of activity (units)	400	650	800	900
Total cost (£)	6,200	6,950	7,400	7,700

First we identify the lowest and highest totals, which are:

£6,200 for 400 units and £7,700 for 900 units.

To calculate the variable cost per unit, we use the fact that the extra cost has been caused by the variable cost of the extra units. That is:

	Cost		**Units**	
High	£7,700		900	
Low	£6,200		400	
Difference	£1,500	÷	500	= £3 per unit

Using £3 per unit, we then calculate the variable part of the cost for 400 units:

£3 x 400 = £1,200

But the total cost for 400 units is £6,200

Therefore the fixed part (which is the same for any number of units)

= £6,200 – £1,200 = £5,000

We can now check the solution by calculating the total cost for 900 units, using our answers:

Total cost = Fixed cost + (variable cost per unit x number of units)

= £5,000 + (£3 x 900)

= £5,000 + £2,700

= £7,700 which agrees with the original data.

The following graph illustrates the behaviour of the total cost in this Case Study. The variable cost per unit determines the gradient (slope) of the line, and the fixed cost is shown where the line cuts the vertical axis. The total costs for 650 units and 800 units lie exactly on the line, but in some cases the points between the high and low may not fit exactly. The high-low method still gives useful information provided that the cost behaviour is approximately semi-variable – that is provided that all the points are approximately in a straight line.

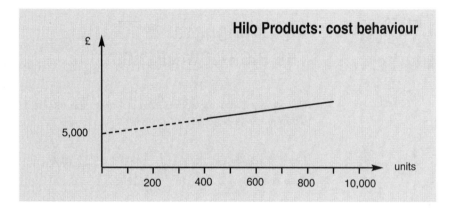

Now check your understanding of this subject by reading through the summary below and following through the practical worked example which follows.

---

high-low method summary

1 identify the highest and lowest cost totals and their levels of activity

2 calculate the difference between the two cost totals

3 calculate the difference in cost units between the two levels of activity

4 divide the difference in cost by the difference in units: this gives the variable cost per unit

5 use the variable cost per unit to calculate the variable part of one of the cost totals

6 deduct the variable part from the cost total to obtain the fixed part

7 check the answers by using them to calculate the other cost total, which should agree with the given data

worked example

required

Calculate the fixed and variable parts of the semi-variable cost which behaves as follows:

Total cost for 6,400 units is £136,000

Total cost for 9,900 units is £162,250

solution

•	Only two levels are given, high and low		
•	Difference in total cost	= £162,250 – £136,000	= £26,250
•	Difference in number of units	= 9,900 – 6,400	= 3,500
•	Variable cost per unit	= £26,250 ÷ 3,500	= £7.50
•	Variable part for 6,400 units	= £7.50 x 6,400	= £48,000
•	Fixed part	= £136,000 – £48,000	= £88,000
•	Check your answer	£88,000 + (£7.50 x 9,900)	= £162,250

FUNCTIONAL ORGANISATION AND REPORTING

Organisations are managed as a group of different functions – for example 'Production' (for a manufacturing organisation), 'Sales and Distribution', 'Administration', and 'Finance'. This structure is illustrated in the sample organisation chart shown below. These functions can also be sub-divided into areas of control according to the needs of the organisation.

As well as each of these functions being controlled by individual managers, the accounting systems (both financial and management) will have been developed to operate with the same structure. As an important part of the management accounting system, budgeting will use the functional structure, and budgets will be developed within the functions and reporting carried out to the functional managers.

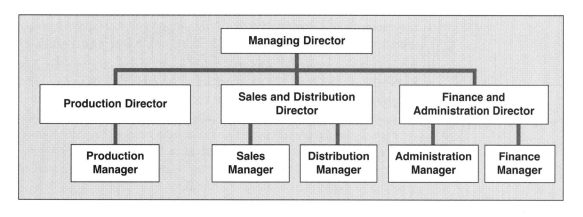

The term '**responsibility accounting**' is used to describe a way of looking at an organisation in terms of areas of responsibility, which could be functions or parts of functions. Such areas of responsibility are called **responsibility centres**.

An individual manager can then be held accountable for certain aspects of the performance of the particular function for which he or she is responsible.

Which aspects of performance should a particular manager have to account for? Clearly, in a fair system, these would be those aspects which they can actually do something about, or over which they have some influence. This brings us to the concept of **controllability**, which is explained in more detail in the next section.

In order to be able to influence the outcomes of a responsibility centre, the manager must have the authority to take the necessary actions. Within a large organisation, there will be various levels of management from the senior executives to supervisors of small departments, each with an appropriate level of authority.

For example, the chief executive may have the authority to sign a contract for a major capital investment project, whereas a production manager has the authority to organise the week's production scheduling.

The extent of a person's authority is clearly linked to the area for which they can be held responsible. There are three categories of responsibility centre which are linked to different levels of authority:

- A **cost centre** (or expense centre) is a responsibility centre where the manager has responsibility for costs. The manager has the authority to take certain actions in relation to the control of costs.

  For example, an office manager can authorise the purchase of stationery and introduce controls to reduce wastage of paper.

- A **profit centre** is a responsibility centre where the manager has responsibility for both costs and income, and hence profit. The manager has the authority to take action relating to income as well as costs.

  For example, the manager of a branch office of an estate agent may have the authority to negotiate levels of commission with clients (perhaps within a specified range), as well as deciding on advertising expenditure.

- An **investment centre** is a responsibility centre where the manager has responsibility for costs, income and some investments. The manager's authority is as for a profit centre, with the additional authority to buy and sell assets, up to certain limits. The manager therefore has some influence over the capital employed in this section of the organisation and Return on Capital Employed could be used as a measure of management performance. We will discuss Return on Capital Employed and other measures of performance later in this book.

For example, the manager of a division which makes some of the products of a large manufacturing company may have the authority to buy and sell machinery up to a given value.

budget centres as areas of responsibility

A **budget centre** is a department, activity or function for which a budget is prepared and the person who is responsible for implementing that budget is the **budget holder**. We will examine the range of budgets and how they are controlled in more detail in Chapter 3.

In order to implement a budget, the budget holder must have sufficient authority to take the necessary actions, and can then be held responsible for the performance of the budget centre in comparison with the budget. Each budget centre is therefore a responsibility centre and may be any of three types of centre described above:

- a budget centre which is a cost (or expense) centre would have a budget for costs (or expenses) only
- a budget centre which is a profit centre would have a budget for both costs and incomes
- a budget centre which is an investment centre would have a budget for costs, incomes and capital expenditure

When the performance of a department, activity or function is measured against the budget, it is important to apply the principle of comparing like with like, and also to measure only those aspects of performance which the budget holder is able do something about. These are the aspects which are described as controllable for that person, as explained below.

controllable costs and incomes

A particular cost or income is described as 'controllable' by a particular person if that person is in a position to influence it. It does not necessarily mean that the person has absolute control over it.

For example, the total cost of wages in a department can be said to be controllable by the manager of the department if he (or she) has the authority to decide how many staff of each grade to employ. However, the manager may not have absolute control over the total wage bill, because the rates of pay may be set at levels which he cannot change. The manager can influence the total wages and therefore it can be considered as being within his area of responsibility.

Whether something is controllable or not depends on the individual manager being considered, in terms of the post which they occupy and the level of responsibility that goes with it. Every cost or income can be influenced by someone in the organisation with a sufficiently high level of authority.

Factors such as bank interest rates, foreign exchange, inflation and so on are not controllable, but the costs affected by these factors can be influenced by management decisions.

For example, the cost of borrowing money is affected by interest rates, but decisions relating to amounts of borrowing and sources of finance can influence the total cost.

Controllability of costs or incomes is important for performance measurement, because clearly it would be unfair and demotivating to measure people's performance on something over which they have no influence.

Controllability of costs or incomes links to the idea of responsibility accounting: if managers have clearly defined areas of responsibility, where they can influence the costs or incomes or both, then they can be held responsible for those costs or incomes and their performance can be measured on the results.

The fairest ways of measuring performance would therefore be:

- On **controllable costs** in a cost centre – a possible method of measurement is variance analysis. The cost centre manager should not have to account for variances on costs which he cannot influence, for example apportionments of fixed overheads.

- On **controllable profit** in a profit centre – profit margin or contribution to sales ratio, as well as variance analysis, could be used for measurement, again applying the principle of excluding items which cannot be influenced by the manager, if possible. Difficulties arise because the exact boundaries between what can and cannot be influenced are not always completely clear cut: for example, by how much does a quality improvement affect sales volumes?

- On **return on capital employed** in an investment centre – here, the calculation of profit and of capital employed may be based where possible on controllable items. However, capital provided by the organisation as a whole and which is not controllable by the centre manager may be taken into account. This allows measurement of how well the total capital employed has been used by the manager to generate profits.

Chapter Summary

■ Management Accounting is guided by its usefulness to managers, and has no external rules or formats that must be followed.

■ Budgets are based around the organisation's costing system, which can be derived from Absorption Costing, Marginal Costing, or Activity Based Costing. Each system uses different terminology and different ways of calculating the cost of an organisation's output or activities. The different ways that inventory can be valued in management accounts affects the amount of profit that is recorded in each period when inventory levels change.

■ Cost behaviour relates to the way that costs change when activity levels change. The main ways that costs behave are as fixed costs, variable costs, semi-variable costs and step costs. The high-low method can be used to split semi-variable costs into their elements.

■ Responsibility accounting involves collecting and reporting information regarding individual managers' areas of responsibility. This is carried out through the use of cost centres, profit centres and investment centres within functional areas.

Key Terms

financial accounting the branch of accounting that is concerned with reporting performance to those outside the organisation

management accounting the branch of accounting that is concerned with providing useful information to managers within the organisation. This book is concerned with some of the main aspects of Management Accounting

absorption costing this is a system that attempts to determine a 'full' production cost for each unit of output. It therefore includes both direct and indirect costs, and uses the mechanisms of allocation, apportionment and absorption to incorporate the indirect production costs

marginal costing this costing system categorises costs according to their cost behaviour, and divides them into variable and fixed costs. This system uses a cost for each unit of output based purely on the variable (or 'marginal') costs. All fixed costs are regarded as time based and are therefore linked to accounting periods rather than units of output

activity based costing

this is a development of absorption costing, and uses a more sophisticated system to deal with the indirect costs. This involves examining indirect costs to determine what causes them, and using this information to charge the costs to the units of output in an appropriate manner

responsibility accounting

the division of an organisation and its reporting into areas of responsibility called responsibility centres; responsibility centres include cost centres, profit centres and investment centres

cost behaviour

the ways that total costs change when the activity level changes; examples are fixed costs, variable costs, semi-variable costs and step costs

Activities

1.1 A manufacturing company which makes a single product has the following annual budgeted costs:

	£
Direct materials	240,000
Direct labour	180,000
Fixed production overheads	600,000
Fixed non-production overheads	120,000
Variable selling costs	24,000

The normal budgeted production per year is 48,000 units. Direct materials and direct labour costs behave as variable costs.

Select the correct absorption cost per unit and marginal cost per unit from the following lists:

Absorption cost per unit		Marginal cost per unit	
(a) £24.25		(a) £8.75	
(b) £21.25		(b) £11.25	
(c) £12.50		(c) £11.75	
(d) £23.75		(d) £9.25	

1.2 The System Company manufactures one product, the Tem. Budgeted production is 4,000 Tems per week. During each of the first two weeks of this year it had costs as follows, exactly as budgeted.

Direct Materials   £5,000

Direct Labour   £9,000

Fixed Overheads   £6,000

The company had no finished goods in stock at the start of week 1. In both weeks it produced 4,000 units. Sales in week 1 were 3,000 units, and in week 2 were 5,000 units, all at £8 per Tem.

Both Direct Materials and Direct Labour behave as Variable Costs.

(a) Produce profit statements for each of the two weeks, using:

(1) Absorption costing, absorbing fixed overheads on a per unit basis

(2) Marginal costing

(b) Explain briefly the reason for the difference between recorded profits under the alternative costing systems.

1.3 The Radical Company produces a variety of goods, according to customers' demands. Some items have been produced to the same specification for many years, while others are constantly updated to meet the needs of the consumers. Some products have long production runs, while others are produced in small batches for specific customers.

Explain whether you believe that Absorption Costing, Marginal Costing, or Activity Based Costing would appear to be most appropriate for this company.

1.4 Select an appropriate accounting treatment for each of the following costs:

- Holiday pay for production workers
- Material wastage in production
- Cost of the purchasing department
- Administrative wages
- Computing services
- Production equipment maintenance
- Depreciation of production equipment
- Redecoration of the sales showroom

Options available are:

- Allocate to marketing overheads
- Allocate to administrative overheads
- Direct cost
- Charge to production in a machine hour overhead rate
- Charge to production in a labour hour overhead rate
- Activity based charge to production cost centres

1.5 Calculate the appropriate budgeted overhead recovery rate for the following production department. The department's annual budget for indirect costs is:

	£
Indirect labour	25,500
Supervisor wages	28,500
Depreciation of equipment	6,000
Machine maintenance	5,250
Canteen subsidy	9,750
Total	75,000

Note: The budget production of 3,750 units will require 7,500 machine hours and 37,500 direct labour hours.

Complete the following:

Overhead recovery should be based on **Labour hours / Machine hours.**

The recovery rate will be £ . . . . per . . . .

1.6 For this task, assume that the cost of power is a semi-variable cost.

(a) Using the high-low method, calculate the fixed cost and the variable cost per unit for power from the following data:

Month	Total cost of power	Level of activity
1	£51,000	90,000 units produced
2	£43,000	70,000 units produced
3	£59,000	110,000 units produced

(b) Using your answers to (a), calculate the expected total cost of power if 80,000 units are produced.

1.7   A company hires punching machines to carry out activities in its production department. Each machine can deal with up to 5,000 units per month. The hire charge for each punching machine is £600 per month. The budgeted volume of units to be made each month is shown in the following table.

Complete the table to show the budgeted monthly machine hire costs.

Month	Budgeted Output (Units)	Budgeted Hire Costs
1	6,000	
2	8,000	
3	4,500	
4	9,000	
5	11,000	

2 Forecasting techniques

this chapter covers...

In this chapter we will examine some useful forecasting techniques that can be applied when budgeting. Since management accounting is forward looking it is important that we can use a variety of techniques to ensure that we have valid data to back up our forecasts.

We firstly review the sources of information and data that can be useful for management accounting. We then look at the way that sampling can be used to collect data. This is often used for market research, which is a useful tool for collecting data about our products and services that can be used to build budgets.

We then go on to study time series analysis – the use of numerical data that occurs over time. This can be used to help forecast the future if it is believed that it will follow historical trends. We include here a study of seasonal variations and their impact on data.

The next section is concerned with forecasting prices and costs. Both percentage calculations and the use of index numbers are examined with numerous examples.

The final section examines factors that can influence forecasts. The product life cycle and the way that pricing affects sales at various stages is discussed. The way that external factors can be identified using 'PEST' analysis is also explained.

FORECASTING TECHNIQUES

Forecasting is often carried out at the start of the budgeting cycle, as we will discuss further in the next chapter. Forecasting is concerned with using data to estimate what will happen in the future. Budgeting involves committing to plans that are based on actions that will be taken. These plans will take into account the information from the forecasts.

An analogy sometimes used is that a weather forecast will predict (for example) whether it will rain or not. Our plan (or budget) will be based on what we intend to do to in response to the forecast – for example, will we take an umbrella?

The techniques described below can be used to help make forecasts. The techniques involve the collection and the analysis of data to provide useful information.

primary and secondary data

Where data is collected specifically for analysis undertaken at that time by an organisation, then the data is known as 'primary data'. Where the data has been collected and provided by another organisation then it is known as 'secondary data'. For example, if a business analyses its sales figures, that is primary data; if it uses inflation figures provided by the Government's statistical services, that is secondary data.

The following table gives examples of specific sources, the kind of information that may be available, and what it could be used for. The list is not intended to be exhaustive, so you can probably think of further examples.

external sources and uses of information (mainly secondary data)		
Source	**Information**	**Use**
Government Statistics	• Forecast Inflation, Economic Growth, Social trends	• Planning Future Activities
Financial Press	• Competitors' Performance • Forecast Interest Rates	• Comparison and Resulting Action
World Wide Web	• Information and Commentary on Most Issues	• Planning Future Activities
Trade Associations	• Typical Performance in the Trade	• Comparison and Resulting Action
Market Research	• Views of Prospective Customers	• Planning Future Activities
Suppliers' Price Lists and Quotations	• Current and Future Costs	• Planning Future Activities

internal sources and uses of information (mainly primary data)

Source	Information	Use
Purchase Invoices	• Quantity and Cost of Goods Purchased	• Costing Current and Future Output of Organisation
Wages Analysis	• Time and Cost of Labour	• Costing Current and Future Output of Organisation
Work Study Reports	• Labour Time to Undertake Activities	• Standard Costs of Output
Unfulfilled Sales Orders	• Type and Quantity of Output Demand	• Planning Future Output
Payables (Creditors) Accounts	• Amounts Owed and When Due	• Planning Future Payments
Inventory (Stock) Records	• Quantity of Goods in Stock & Ordered	• Planning Future Purchases
Production Schedules	• Type and Quantity of Output Planned	• Planning Resource Requirements
Quality Control Records	• Number of Items Rejected	• Monitoring Input and Output
H.R. (Human Resources) Reports	• Current and Future Employee and Pay Data	• Planning Future Labour Resources and Costs

census or sample?

If we want to collect data about a population (not just a population of people, but any large group of items or data) there are two approaches that we could use.

■ A **census** could be used to collect data about every item in the population. One example of this technique is the Government's 10 yearly census of all the people in the UK. This provides information which can be used by the Government to plan services. A census provides a complete picture of the 'population', but is expensive, and will often be impractical.

■ **Sampling** is a commonly used technique for collecting data from a small number within a 'population', to estimate information regarding the whole 'population'. Market research questionnaires are an example of sampling. Sampling is cheaper to carry out than a full census, but it must be carried out carefully if the results are to be used with confidence.

SAMPLING

The critical issue to consider when examining sampling techniques is that the sample must be as free from bias as practical. If you wanted to estimate the faults in the whole production output of a factory it would not make sense to only sample the output of a machine manned by a trainee on his first day at work!

Some common uses of sampling are to estimate:

■ customer satisfaction levels

■ quality of production output

■ the views of prospective customers (market research)

There are various approaches to sampling. The approach taken will depend on the type of population and the resources available. The approach will influence the reliability of the estimates produced.

random sampling

This is the approach that will provide the best estimate. It is based on the rule that every item in the population has an equal chance of being selected. In order for this to happen the exact size of the population must be known, and a 'sampling frame' created by numbering every item. From this frame the sample can be selected using random numbers. This approach could be used (for example) as a way of sampling current customers to find out their views on our products. This is assuming the whole population (the number of current customers) would be known from the outset. It could not be used to ascertain the views of bald men in Bradford because there is no way of accurately knowing how many there are and who they are.

quasi-random sampling

This approach contains a number of techniques that can provide a good approximation to random sampling. Although they are not quite as accurate as random sampling, they can produce similar outcomes, often using fewer resources. The techniques are:

■ **Systematic Sampling**
  Choosing every 'n'th item after a random start. For example selecting customers by starting at customer number 63, and then obtaining the views of every 17th customer from there.

■ **Stratified Sampling**
  Dividing the population into groups ('strata' means 'layers'), and then choosing a sample from each of the strata based on its size. For example customers could be grouped according to their location. If there were

more customers in London than in Devon then the sample for London would be larger. Each group would be sampled independently in this way in proportion to its size.

---

worked example

A company has a total of 5,000 customers, located in Devon (500 customers), Surrey (1,500 customers) and London (3,000 customers). It wishes to sample a total of 200 of these customers to obtain their views. The sample of 200 customers would be divided into the three locations based on the split of the total customers over the locations, as follows:

	Total	Devon	Surrey	London
Total Customers	5,000	500	1,500	3,000
Sample	200	20	60	120

The calculation for the Devon sample size is (500 / 5,000) x 200. Other calculations follow the same procedure.

■ **Multistage Sampling**

Dividing the 'population' into groups, and then randomly selecting several groups as an initial sample. These selected groups are then sub-divided and sub groups randomly chosen (the procedure may be repeated several times). For example customers could be divided into groups based on their location, and the groups of Yorkshire, Sussex and Cornwall randomly selected. Within each group towns could then be chosen at random (for example Halifax, Brighton and Truro), and the customer sample selected from within these areas.

non-random sampling

This approach must be used when a sampling frame cannot be established (for example because the size of the population is not known). The results generated by this approach will typically be less reliable than random or quasi-random approaches, but are nevertheless useful. These techniques are often used for market research.

■ **Quota Sampling**

Restricting the sample to a fixed number per strata. For example interviewing people in the street within certain categories (for example age groups, gender etc) until a predetermined number have been interviewed.

■ **Cluster Sampling**

Selecting one subsection of the population as representative, and just sampling that. For example interviewing dog owners who live in Cardiff as being representative of dog owners throughout the UK.

USE OF FORECASTING TECHNIQUES

Forecasting is used in budget setting in two main ways:

1 The **key budget factor** will need to be forecast as accurately as possible to provide data that the various budgets can be built upon. This is often the sales level for a commercial organisation, but it could be other factors, such as production capacity.

2 The **other data** in the various budgets may be subject to various forecasts. These could include forecasts of inflation that would affect all the budgets to some extent, along with other more specific forecasts, for example currency movements or interest rates.

The forecasting of the key (or principal) budget factor data is the most important part of the whole budgeting process, and yet is often the most difficult task to carry out. How does a business know, for example, how well its products will sell? Maybe a competitor will dent its sales, maybe the business will come up with an unexpected best-seller.

Techniques that can be used to assist in the forecasting process range from purely numerical methods like trend analysis using seasonal variations, to estimates that can amount to little more than informed guesses. In practice a combination of methods may be used.

For any technique that is based on using past data to produce useful forecasts of the future, the future must in some way depend upon the past. But there is always a danger of assuming that a trend will continue to travel in the same direction that it has done for the last few years. In reality there may be a massive change in direction about to happen caused by something that we did not know about or did not consider to be relevant.

As mentioned earlier, it is important that any forecasts are made available for relevant managers to raise queries and seek clarification. This will need to be carried out regardless of the specific technique that is used to develop the forecast initially.

The techniques used in sales forecasting include **trend analysis**, **market research** and the use of **consulting experts**.

trend analysis

At its simplest, trend analysis can mean assuming that sales will continue to move in the same direction and rate as they have in the recent past. Often seasonal variations are isolated from the historical data to produce 'deseasonalised' data that can be used as a basis for the forecast of the trend, before anticipated seasonal variations are added back in. This method cannot account for random movements in the data that may be a significant part of the data. The method also relies on there being suitable historical data available, so is not always appropriate.

market research

Market research may be an appropriate starting point, and is particularly suitable for new or revised products or services. Market research can make use of published statistics (eg economic and social trends) or it can involve a direct approach to the marketplace using techniques such as questionnaires and focus groups. Great care must be taken to ensure that the sampling system provides data that is as free from bias as is practical. There will be costs and benefits applicable to methods ranging from postal or telephone questionnaires to focus groups and street interviews. A balance must be struck between the method used, the sample size, the accuracy required, and the cost involved. Users must be aware of the level of reliance that they can place on the data generated.

consulting experts

An organisation can build up a forecast by assessing the estimates of experts. Rather than making assumptions about overall sales levels, this method combines the estimates of those with local knowledge and experience. For example a business can ask individual sales representatives or sales outlets to forecast their expected sales levels, and then combine the results. This should have the advantage of utilising the knowledge of those aware of local conditions, but could be subject to personal bias and prejudices. Also, the experts providing the estimates may not be aware of wider economic issues that could affect the data. Major customers could also provide data by giving estimates of their requirements, or some form of questionnaire could be sent out to provide an estimate of all established customers' needs.

TIME SERIES ANALYSIS

Time series analysis involves analysing numerical trends over a time period. It is often used to examine past and present trends so that future trends can be forecast. The term 'trend analysis' is used to describe the technique that we will now examine. At its simplest the concept is based on the assumption that data will continue to move in the same direction in the future as it has in the past.

Using the sales of a shoe shop as an example we will now look a range of techniques of dealing with trends.

an identical annual change

A shoe shop 'Comfy Feet' has sold the following numbers of pairs of shoes annually over the last few years:

20-1	10,000
20-2	11,000
20-3	12,000
20-4	13,000
20-5	14,000
20-6	15,000
20-7	16,000

It does not require a great deal of arithmetic to calculate that if the trend continues at the previous rate – an increase of 1,000 pairs a year – then shoe sales could be forecast at 17,000 pairs in 20-8 and 18,000 pairs in 20-9. Of course this is a very simple example, and life is rarely this straightforward. For example, for how long can this rate of increase be sustained?

average annual change

A slightly more complex technique could have been used to arrive at the same answer for the shoe shop. If we compare the number of sales in 20-7 with the number in 20-1, we can see that it has risen by 6,000 pairs. By dividing that figure by the number of times the year changed in our data we can arrive at an average change per year. The number of times that the year changes is 6, which is the same as the number of 'spaces' between the years (or alternatively the total number of years minus 1).

Shown as an equation this becomes:

Average Annual Sales Change =

$$\frac{(Sales\ in\ Last\ Year - Sales\ in\ First\ Year)}{(Number\ of\ Years - 1)} = \frac{(16,000 - 10,000)}{(7 - 1)}$$

= + 1,000, which is what we would expect.

The + 1,000 would then be added to the sales data in 20-7 of 16,000 (the last actual data) to arrive at a forecast of 17,000.

This technique is useful when all the increases are not quite identical, yet we want to use the average increase to forecast the trend. A negative answer would show that the average change is a reduction, not an increase. We will use this technique when estimating the trend movement in more complicated situations.

This is not the only way that we can estimate the direction that data is moving over time, and it does depend on the data (including especially the first and last points) falling roughly into a straight line. We will note alternative methods that can be used later in this section.

constructing a graph

The same result can be produced graphically. Using the same shoe shop example we can extend the graph based on the actual data to form a forecast line.

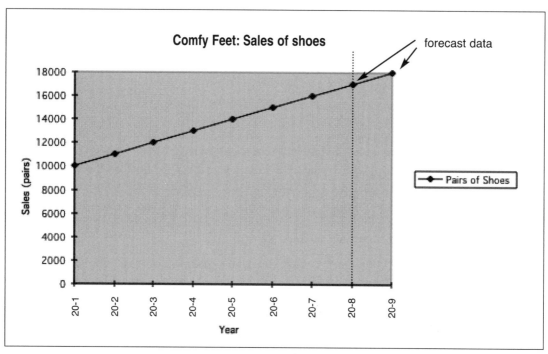

If, in another situation, the actual data does not produce exactly equal increases, the graph will produce the same answer as the average annual change provided the straight line runs through the first and last year's data points.

using a formula

The data in the example could have been expressed in the following formula:

$$y = mx + c$$

where:

y is the forecast amount

m is 1,000 (the amount by which the data increases each year)

x is the number of years since the start year (20-1)

c is 10,000 (which is the sales figure in the start year of 20-1)

If we wanted a forecast for the year 20-9, we could calculate it as:

Forecast   = (1,000 x number of years since 20-1) + 10,000

y (the forecast) = (1,000 x 8) + 10,000

                  = 18,000, which is what we would expect.

This formula works because the formula is based on the equation of a straight line.

linear regression

In the last section on time series analysis we saw that when some historical data moves in a consistent and regular way over time we can use it to help estimate the future trend of that data. We also saw that in these circumstances the data can be represented by:

- a straight line on a graph, and / or
- an equation of the line in the form $y = mx + c$

to help us develop the trend.

Linear regression is the term used for the techniques that can be used to determine the line that best replicates that given data. You should be aware of the techniques in general terms, and be able to appreciate their usefulness. In an assessment you may be given historical data or the equation of a line and asked to use it to generate a forecast.

Where data exactly matches a straight line (as with the 'Comfy Feet' data) there is no need to use any special techniques. In other situations the following could be used:

- **Average annual change**. This method was described earlier, and is useful if we are confident that the first and last points (taken chronologically since we are looking at data over time) are both representative. It will smooth out any minor fluctuations of the data in-between.

- **Line of best fit**. Where the data falls only roughly into a straight line, but the first and last points do not appear to be very representative the average annual change method would give a distorted solution. Here a line of best fit can be drawn onto the data points on a graph that will form a better estimate of the movement of the data. The following graph illustrates a situation where the line of best fit would provide a better solution than the average annual change method.

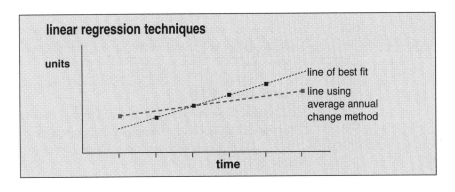

■ **Least squares method**. This is a mathematical technique for developing the equation of the most appropriate line. It is more accurate than drawing a line of best fit onto a graph by eye, but the calculations involved are outside the scope of the learning area covered in this book.

All linear regression techniques assume that a straight line is an appropriate representation of the data. When looking at time series this means that we are assuming that the changes in the data that we are considering (known as the dependent variable) are in proportion to the movement of time (the independent variable). This would mean that we are expecting (for example) the sales level to continually rise over time. When we use time series analysis later in the book we must remember that sometimes data does not travel forever in a straight line, even though they may do so for a short time. For example share prices on the stock market do not continue to go up (or down) steadily, but often move in a more erratic way.

The ideas behind regression analysis apply not only to time series analysis, but can be used in many other situations, for example, earlier in this book, examining the behaviour of semi-variable costs at different activity levels. The 'high-low' method was used to split costs between their fixed and variable components. This method uses an identical principle to the 'average annual change' method described above.

The data that is used for analysis in various situations may be the result of using sampling techniques (as outlined earlier in this chapter). In that case the reliance that can be placed on the outcomes of our analysis will depend not only on the regression analysis, but also on the validity of the sampling techniques used.

TIME SERIES ANALYSIS AND SEASONAL VARIATIONS

There are four main factors that can influence data which is generated over a period of time:

■ **The underlying trend**

This is the way that the data is generally moving in the long term. For example the volume of traffic on our roads is generally increasing as time goes on.

■ **Long term cycles**

These are slow moving variations that may be caused by economic cycles or social trends. For example, when economic prosperity generally increases this may increase the volume of traffic as more people own cars and fewer use buses. In times of economic depression there may be a decrease in car use as people cannot afford to travel as much or may not have employment which requires them to travel.

- **Seasonal variations**

  This term refers to regular, predictable cycles in the data. The cycles may or may not be seasonal in the normal use of the term (eg spring, summer etc). For example, traffic volumes are always higher in the daytime, especially on weekdays, and lower at weekends and at night.

- **Random variations**

  All data will be affected by influences that are unpredictable. For example, flooding of some roads may reduce traffic volume along that route, but increase it on alternative routes. Similarly the traffic volume may be influenced by heavy snowfall.

The type of numerical problems that you are most likely to face in assessments will tend to ignore the effects of long-term cycles (which will effectively be considered as a part of the trend) and random variations (which are impossible to forecast). We are therefore left with analysing data into underlying trends and seasonal variations, in order to create forecasts.

The technique that we will use follows the process in this diagram:

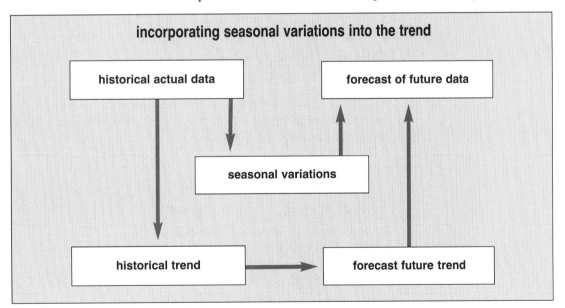

The process is as follows:

1 The historical actual data is analysed into the historical trend and the seasonal variations.

2 The historical trend is used to forecast the future trend, using the techniques examined in the last section.

3 The seasonal variations are incorporated with the forecast future trend to provide a forecast of where the actual data will be in the future.

analysing historical actual data

In a task the analysis may have been carried out already, or you may be asked to carry out the analysis by using 'moving averages'. If you are using moving averages it is important that:

- your workings are laid out accurately

- the number of pieces of data that are averaged corresponds with the number of 'seasons' in a cycle

- where there is an even number of 'seasons' in a cycle a further averaging of each pair of averages takes place

how do moving averages work?

A moving average is the term used for a series of averages calculated from a stream of data so that:

- every average is based on the same number of pieces of data, (eg four pieces of data in a 'four-point moving average'), and

- each subsequent average moves along that data stream by one piece of data so that compared to the previous average it

  - uses one new piece of data and

  - abandons one old piece of data

This is easier to calculate than it sounds! For example, suppose we had a list of six pieces of data relating to the factory output over two days where a three-shift pattern was worked as follows:

Day 1	Morning Shift	14 units
	Afternoon Shift	20 units
	Night Shift	14 units
Day 2	Morning Shift	26 units
	Afternoon Shift	32 units
	Night Shift	26 units

If we thought that the shift being worked might influence the output, we could calculate a three-point moving average. The workings would be as follows:

First moving average: $(14 + 20 + 14) \div 3 = 16$

Second moving average: $(20 + 14 + 26) \div 3 = 20$

Third moving average: $(14 + 26 + 32) \div 3 = 24$

Fourth moving average $(26 + 32 + 26) \div 3 = 28$

Notice how we move along the list of data. In this simple example with six pieces of data we can't work out any more three-point averages since we have arrived at the end of the numbers after only four calculations.

Here we chose the number of pieces of data to average each time so that it corresponded with the number of points in a full cycle. By choosing a three-point moving average that corresponded with the number of shifts we always had **one** example of the output of **every** type of shift in our average. This means that any influence on the average by including a night shift (for example) is cancelled out by also including data from a morning shift and an afternoon shift.

We must be careful to always work out moving averages so that exactly one complete cycle is included in every average. The number of 'points' is chosen to suit the data.

When determining a trend line, each average relates to the data from its mid point, as the following layout of the figures just calculated demonstrates.

		Output	**Trend (Moving Average)**
Day 1	Morning Shift	14 units	
	Afternoon Shift	20 units	16 units
	Night Shift	14 units	20 units
Day 2	Morning Shift	26 units	24 units
	Afternoon Shift	32 units	28 units
	Night Shift	26 units	

This means that the first average that we calculated (16 units) can be used as the trend point of the afternoon shift on day 1, with the second point (20 units) forming the trend point of the night shift on day 1. The result is that we:

■ know exactly where the trend line is for each period of time, and

■ have a basis from which we can calculate 'seasonal variations'

Even using our limited data in this example we can see how seasonal variations can be calculated. *A seasonal variation is simply the difference between the actual data at a point and the trend at the same point*. This gives us the seasonal variations shown in the following table, using the figures already calculated.

		Output	**Trend**	**Seasonal Variation**
Day 1	Morning Shift	14 units		
	Afternoon Shift	20 units	16 units	+4 units
	Night Shift	14 units	20 units	–6 units
Day 2	Morning Shift	26 units	24 units	+2 units
	Afternoon Shift	32 units	28 units	+4 units
	Night Shift	26 units		

The seasonal variation for the afternoon shift, calculated on day 1, is based on the actual output being 4 units greater than the trend at the same point (ie 20 minus 16 units).

absolute or percentage seasonal variations?

The examples that we have used so far have used the idea of absolute (or 'additive') seasonal variations – ones that are expressed in the same units as the actual data that is being analysed. Sometimes a more accurate forecast can be obtained when the seasonal variations are expressed as a percentage of the trend. This would make sense when the variations naturally become greater as the trend increases. This could occur, for example, if we were analysing the cost of domestic heating over a number of years: as the trend increased (due to cost inflation) the differences between the summer and winter heating costs would also increase at about the same rate.

Case Study

UK ICE CREAM CONSUMPTION

An investigation into the quarterly amount an average UK household spends on ice cream has revealed an underlying trend and percentage variations as follows.

Each quarter the trend increased by £1, and by quarter 4 of 20-2 it had reached £50 per quarter.

The seasonal variations, based on percentages of the trend in that quarter, were calculated as:

Quarter 1	−70%		
Quarter 2	+40%		
Quarter 3	+60%		
Quarter 4	−30%		

required

Forecast the average quarterly spend on ice cream per household in each quarter of 20-5.

solution

The calculation here is straightforward. Note that quarter 1 of 20-5 is 9 quarters later than the quarter that we already know the trend for, ie quarter 4 of 20-2.

		Forecast Trend		Seasonal Variations	Forecast
20-5	Qtr 1	£50 + (9 x £1)	= £59	− 70%	£17.70
	Qtr 2	£50 + (10 x £1)	= £60	+ 40%	£84.00
	Qtr 3	£50 + (11 x £1)	= £61	+ 60%	£97.60
	Qtr 4	£50 + (12 x £1)	= £62	− 30%	£43.40

FORECASTING PRICES AND COSTS

percentage calculations

Percentages are used in various calculations for budgeting, and although they are fairly straightforward it is still worth making sure that we can deal with them.

The most basic percentage calculation required is when an amount that is expressed as a percentage needs to be added to (or deducted from) an original figure.

worked example

The labour cost this year is £2,150,000.
The budget for this cost next year needs to allow for a 4% increase.

4% of £2,150,000 is calculated as:

4/100 x £2,150,000 = £86,000.

The £86,000 is then added to the £2,150,000 to give £2,236,000.

Alternatively, we could calculate it as £2,150,000 x 104/100 = £2,236,000.

The sort of calculation that can cause problems is when we are working back to change an earlier percentage calculation. Here we need to be careful.

worked example

The labour cost budget has been calculated as £2,236,000 based on a 4% increase (as in the last example). The original figure is not provided. Now we are asked to calculate alternative budget figures, based on:

(a)   no 4% increase, and

(b)   a 2.5% increase instead of the 4% increase

solution

(a)   To carry out the calculation we must remember that the £2,236,000 is 104% of the original figure. We therefore need to reduce our figure by 4/104.

        4/104 x £2,236,000   = £86,000

        £2,236,000 – £86,000   = £2,150,000

(b)   Using the original figure of £2,150,000 that we have just calculated, it is now a simple matter to add 2.5% of £2,150,000 to it.

        2.5/100 x £2,150,000   = £53,750

        £53,750 + £2,150,000   = £2,203,750

Note that we cannot arrive at the correct answer by simply deducting 4% for part (a), or deducting 1.5% for part (b).

The same logic applies to percentage reductions, but they can be a little trickier.

worked example

The material budget for next year was provisionally set at £1,843,000, after allowing for a 3% reduction. The reduction is now thought to be only 2.2%.

The new budget figure can be calculated as follows:

Calculate the original figure:

        £1,843,000 x 100/97   = £1,900,000

        (or calculate 3/97 and add this on to £1,843,000)

Calculate the new reduction:

        2.2/100 x £1,900,000   = £41,800

        The £41,800 is then deducted from the £1,900,000 to give £1,858,200.

Some calculations with percentages involve both volumes and costs. Here the overall cost will be found by multiplying the unit cost by the volume. Any percentage changes will similarly be calculated by multiplying the percentages together.

worked example

Suppose materials currently cost £15 per unit, and the quantity currently purchased is 200,000 units. The current cost would be:

  200,000 x £15   = £3,000,000

If the cost is to rise by 3%, and the quantity is to reduce by 1%, then the revised total cost could be calculated as:

  £3,000,000 x 103/100 x 99/100   = £3,059,100

We can confirm that this is the same result as calculating a revised unit cost of £15 x 103/100 = £15.45, and multiplying it by a revised quantity of 200,000 x 99/100 = 198,000, giving £15.45 x 198,000 = £3,059,100.

This means that we can use this technique, even if we don't know the volumes and unit costs. We can also incorporate the earlier technique for working back to make changes to assumptions.

worked example

Suppose the sales budget was calculated based on a 10% increase in volume from last year, together with a 2% price rise. This budget amounted to £2,805,000.

Now a revised budget needs to be calculated based on increased volume from last year of 8%, and increased prices of 1.5%.

First we can calculate what last year's sales were:

  £2,805,000 x 100/110 x 100/102   = £2,500,000

Then we can increase this figure in line with the new assumptions:

  £2,500,000 x 108% x 101.5%   = £2,740,500

index numbers

Index numbers are used to assist in the comparison of numerical data over time. The most commonly used indices are perhaps the Retail Price Index (RPI) and the Consumer Price Index (CPI), that give an indication of inflation by comparing the cost of a group of expenses typically incurred by households in the UK from year-to-year. There are many other types of index numbers that have been created for specific purposes, for example:

- the average wage rate for a particular job, or for all employment
- the average house price either by region or throughout the UK
- the market price of shares (eg the FTSE 100 index)
- the quantities of specific items that are sold or used (eg litres of unleaded petrol)
- the quantities of a group of items that are sold or used (eg litres of all motor fuel)
- the manufactured cost of specific items or a range of items (sometimes called 'factory gate' prices)

Many government indices and other indicators are available at www.statistics.gov.uk. If you have the opportunity, have a look at the enormous range of data that can either be downloaded free, or can be purchased in government publications.

When using published statistics it is important to make sure that they are specific enough to be useful for your purpose. For example, data on the growth in the population of the West of England will be of limited use if you are trying to forecast the sales in a bookshop in Taunton. Of far more use would be details of proposed housing developments within the immediate area, including the numbers of new homes and the type of households that form the developers' target market.

leading and lagging indicators

Some indicators can be classified as 'leading' indicators, whilst others are known as 'lagging' indicators. This means that some indicators naturally give advance warning of changes that may take place later in other indicators. For example, an index that monitors the prices of manufactured goods ('factory gate' prices) will react to changes before they have filtered through to retail price indices. The index of 'factory gate' prices can therefore be considered to be a 'leading' indicator of retail prices, and give early warning of implications of industrial situations.

In a similar way, an index recording the volume of manufactured output from factories will lag behind an index measuring the volume of purchases of raw materials made by industrial buying departments.

weightings of indices

Those indices that are based on information from more than one item will use some form of weighting to make the results meaningful.

For example, while an index measuring the retail price of premium grade unleaded petrol is based on a single product and therefore needs no weighting, this would not be true for a price index for all vehicle fuel. In this case it will require a decision about how much weight (or importance) is to be placed on each component of the index. Here the relative quantities sold of types of fuel (for example unleaded petrol and diesel) would be a logical way to weight the index. This would ensure that if petrol sales were double those for diesel, any price changes in petrol would have twice the impact on the index than a price change in diesel.

As the purchasing habits of consumers change, then the weighting and composition of complicated indices like the Retail Price Index are often changed to reflect this. This will include changes to the weighting of certain items, for example due to the increase in the proportion of household expenditure on holidays. It can also involve the addition or deletion of certain items entirely (for example the inclusion of certain fast foods). You may have seen news items from time to time about the revision of items contained within the RPI or CPI as consumers' tastes change.

calculations using index numbers

Whatever type of index we need to use, the principle is the same. The index numbers represent a convenient way of comparing figures.

For example, the RPI was 100.0 in January 1987 (known as the base year), and was 259.8 in November 2015. The index increase between these two dates (259.8 – 100.0 = 159.8) represents a percentage increase of 159.8 / 100 = 159.8%. It means that average household costs have gone up by 159.8% in that period. The calculation starting from the base year is a little easier than in other cases – because we can simply divide by 100 to get a percentage – but other calculations are not difficult.

If we know what the current (or historical) price is, and also know the index figure at the same point in time, we can calculate the forecast price at another date if we know what the index is expected to be. The calculation is:

$$\text{Forecast Price} \quad = \quad \text{Historical Price} \ \ x \ \ \frac{\text{Forecast Index (at time converting to)}}{\text{Historical Index (at time converting from)}}$$

For example, if the index was 188.5 last month when a commodity was priced at £99.80, we can calculate its forecast price in several months' time if we know that the index is expected to be 193.4 at that time, as follows:

Forecast Price   = £99.80 x 193.4 / 188.5 = £102.39

Here the answer has been rounded to the nearest penny. Make sure that you follow carefully any instructions about rounding, and don't round your figures part way through the calculation – wait until you get to the final answer.

In this example the percentage increase in the index can also be calculated. It is worked out by dividing the change in the index (193.4 – 188.5 = 4.9) by the initial index figure of 188.5, and then multiplying by 100. The calculation is therefore:

(4.9 / 188.5) x 100 = 2.59947%

Another type of calculation that may be required is when you need to strip out the impact of index data to convert data back to 'year 1 prices'. This can be useful for examining sales revenue to see whether changes are simply a result of index changes or whether there is real growth (or contraction).

For example, we may be provided with the following actual sales revenue and index data for a series of years:

	Year 1	Year 2	Year 3	Year 4
Sales Revenue	£36,600	£38,449	41,018	£42,949
Sales Price Index	550.0	570.0	600.0	620.0

To restate the sales revenue in 'year 1 prices' we need to take each actual sales revenue figure and multiply it by:

$$\frac{\textit{Index at time converting to}}{\textit{Index at time converting from}}$$

This is the same principle that we used in the first example – we are just working backwards in time rather than forwards.

The year 1 sales revenue is already at year 1 prices, so doesn't need converting. The calculations for the other years are as follows. We are going to round to the nearest whole £.

Year 2	£38,449 x (550.0 / 570.0)	=	£37,100
Year 3	£41,018 x (550.0 / 600.0)	=	£37,600
Year 4	£42,949 x (550.0 / 620.0)	=	£38,100

We can now see that once the price index changes have been stripped away, there is still an underlying increase in sales revenue of £500 each year. We could use this to help forecast the sales revenue for year 5.

In year 1 prices, year 5 sales revenue can be forecast at £38,100 + £500 = £38,600.

If we also had a forecast index for year 5 (let's assume it is 645.0) we could then forecast the actual sales revenue in year 5 as:

£38,600 x (645.0 / 550.0) = £45,267

Notice that whichever direction we are travelling when carrying out calculations with index numbers, the rule is the same.

'Multiply by the index you are going to, and divide by the index you are coming from.'

Index numbers referring to costs or prices are the most commonly used ones referred to in the units studied in this book. If we want to use cost index numbers to monitor past costs or forecast future ones, then it is best to use as specific an index as possible. This will then provide greater accuracy than a more general index.

For example, if we were operating in the food industry, and wanted to compare our coffee cost movements with the average that the industry had experienced, we should use an index that analyses coffee costs in the food industry. This would be much more accurate than the RPI, and also better than a general cost index for the food industry.

FACTORS INFLUENCING FORECASTS

Common sense tells us that there are events and developments going on locally, nationally and internationally which can affect our forecasts and should therefore be taken into account where possible.

the product life cycle

It is important when forecasting sales volumes to consider the effect of the product life cycle. Products typically go through a number of distinct stages between conception and finally being withdrawn from sale. The stages are:

■ development

■ launch

■ growth

■ maturity

■ decline

These stages are shown on the following graph:

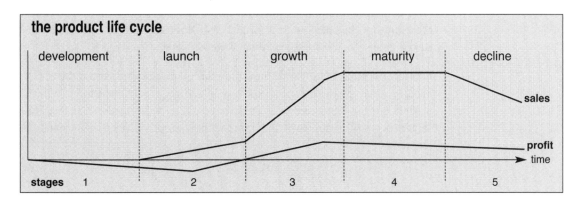

At the beginning of the cycle, development, production and marketing costs are high and so profit may even be negative. If the product is successful, a period of growth follows and sales accelerate up to the level of the maturity stage of the cycle. Here sales have reached a plateau, and demand may be sustained by making product improvements. After the market has become saturated, and virtually all potential buyers satisfied, sales of the product will go into decline. It may be wise to terminate production before all demand has been extinguished to avoid incurring losses, or alternatively repackage and revamp the product.

Marketing strategy during the launch phase of the product life cycle will have an important effect on revenue. One strategy that can work for products that initially have little competition (for example a high quality mobile phone that has unique technological features) is to apply **price skimming**. This involves setting a high initial price which will provide high profit per unit, and this should more than offset low unit sales. In this way it is hoped that development costs can be recovered quickly. The product may be bought by 'early adopters' who want to be seen with the latest products. As competitors launch their products, the price may then need to be reduced to sustain demand.

The opposite launch strategy is to adopt **penetration pricing**. This involves setting a low initial price to encourage a high level of unit sales, although there would be a low profit per unit. The purpose would be to tempt prospective customers who are currently buying from competitors, but who are only modestly satisfied with their purchases. This pricing policy is useful where the product has low development costs that need to be recovered, and it reduces the opportunity for competitors to reduce their prices below yours.

Throughout the product life cycle, the choices made about marketing (the 'marketing mix') will have an important impact on both the sales revenue and the profit.

While some products may move quickly from start-up to decline, others may have a longer life cycle and become what are known as 'cash cows', providing the business with a steady cash flow and source of profitability. Baked beans, for example, have been steady sellers for over 50 years!

It is clearly important to recognise the phases of the cycle, and to be able to identify what phase the products are in to improve forecasting. While a product during the mature phase may have a relatively steady sales level that should be easy to forecast, the approaching period of decline must not be ignored.

PEST analysis

PEST analysis examines:

political

economic

social and

technological factors that affect the performance of a product.

▪ political factors

Governments have control over a variety of issues that can affect future activity levels. For example, importing or exporting can be made more or less attractive by the use of trade tariffs, or joining or leaving exchange rate mechanisms or adopting the Euro. National and international laws affect issues from health & safety to minimum wage levels. Taxation policies will also be important; they affect competing companies and individuals who may be customers.

▪ economic factors

The forecast sales level of organisations must take account of the economy in the market place. If the general economic climate is good, then customers will be more confident about the future. Sales are likely to be higher when fewer people are unemployed, and more money circulates. When the economy deteriorates customers will be more restricted in their spending. The economy is, of course, influenced by political changes, and successive governments have attempted (with varying success) to minimise the large cyclical swings in the economy and promote sustainable growth. Inflation is also closely linked with the economy, and index numbers can be used to record and forecast inflation (as discussed).

▪ social factors

Patterns of individual behaviour, fashions, and perceptions of acceptability and political correctness can all impact on sales. In addition more fundamental changes in the structure of society like the size of the family, divorce levels and the average age at which people have children or retire are clearly important.

▪ technological factors

Technology can affect not only the way that a company manufactures its products, but also the market into which it is selling. A new product announced by a competitor can have a huge impact on sales levels, and the general effect of new technology is continually to shorten the product life cycle.

'FOCUS':
SENSIBLE FORECASTING

situation

A new restaurant called 'Focus' is opened on 1 January. After running for 11 weeks it becomes clear that there is a regular pattern to the number of meals served on different days of the week. The daily variations seem to follow these percentages from the average daily meals sold in that week:

Mondays	−70%
Tuesdays	−50%
Wednesdays	−20%
Thursdays	+30%
Fridays	+40%
Saturdays	+80%
Sundays	−10%

The average number of meals per day served in week one was 20 per day. By week 11 the average had grown to 50 per day. The restaurant manager, Tom Hick, wants an idea of the likely number of meals eaten in 20 weeks' time. He asks you to carry out a number of forecasts but you are dubious about the value of all the methods he suggests and the data you are going to produce. However he is the boss and you have to do what he asks you to do.

required

(a) Using the data provided, forecast the average daily meals to be served in week 31, and the number of meals to be served on the Saturday in that week.

(b) State why you think his idea of a forecast may lack validity. Mention other forecasting factors which might be taken into account.

solution

(a) The average historical trend movement is

$(50 - 20) \div 10$ = +3

ie a rise of 3 average daily meals each week.

Using this trend figure to forecast the average number of meals per day in week 31 results in:

$50 + ([31 - 11] \times 3)$ = 110 average daily meals

This gives a forecast for the Saturday of 110 + 80% of 110 = 198 meals.

(b) A new restaurant would be going through the start-up or growth phase of its life cycle during the weeks for which there is historical data. The trend movement is therefore not sustainable at this level indefinitely, and to assume it will continue for a further 20 weeks may be wildly optimistic.

There are other issues that do not seem to have been considered, including:

- the capacity of the restaurant
- the ability of the staff to maintain quality at higher output levels
- the effect on trade of seasonal variations
- the effect of holiday periods

Chapter Summary

- Data to help forecasting and budgeting can come from various sources, both internal and external.

- Various techniques to help prepare forecasts can be applied when budgeting. Forecasts are estimations of future events that budgets are then created to take account of.

- Sampling can be used to collect data. This is often used for market research, which is a useful tool for collecting data about our products and services that can be used to build budgets.

- Time series analysis is the examination of numerical data that occurs over time. This can be used to help forecast the future if it is believed that it will follow historical trends. It includes the study of seasonal variations and their impact on data.

- Percentage calculations and index numbers can also be used in forecasting. There is a range of indices available and their use will depend on our requirements.

- Factors that influence forecasts include the stage of the product life cycle (and how the product is being marketed) and political, economic, social and technological factors.

Key Terms

sampling

sampling is a commonly used technique for using data about a small number of items within a population, to estimate information regarding the whole population

random sampling

where every item in the population has an equal chance of being selected

systematic sampling

choosing every 'n'th item after a random start

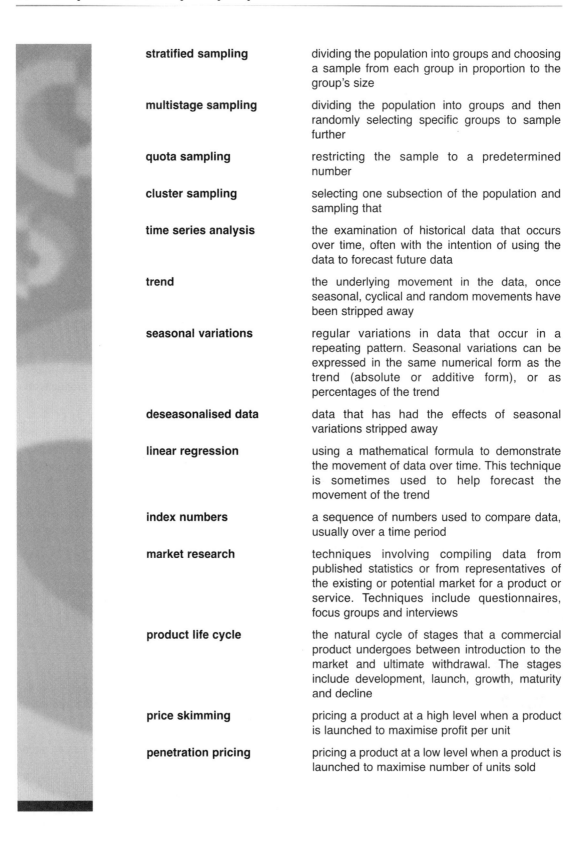

stratified sampling dividing the population into groups and choosing a sample from each group in proportion to the group's size

multistage sampling dividing the population into groups and then randomly selecting specific groups to sample further

quota sampling restricting the sample to a predetermined number

cluster sampling selecting one subsection of the population and sampling that

time series analysis the examination of historical data that occurs over time, often with the intention of using the data to forecast future data

trend the underlying movement in the data, once seasonal, cyclical and random movements have been stripped away

seasonal variations regular variations in data that occur in a repeating pattern. Seasonal variations can be expressed in the same numerical form as the trend (absolute or additive form), or as percentages of the trend

deseasonalised data data that has had the effects of seasonal variations stripped away

linear regression using a mathematical formula to demonstrate the movement of data over time. This technique is sometimes used to help forecast the movement of the trend

index numbers a sequence of numbers used to compare data, usually over a time period

market research techniques involving compiling data from published statistics or from representatives of the existing or potential market for a product or service. Techniques include questionnaires, focus groups and interviews

product life cycle the natural cycle of stages that a commercial product undergoes between introduction to the market and ultimate withdrawal. The stages include development, launch, growth, maturity and decline

price skimming pricing a product at a high level when a product is launched to maximise profit per unit

penetration pricing pricing a product at a low level when a product is launched to maximise number of units sold

Activities

2.1   Match the data in the first column with the appropriate source in the second column.

Data	**Source**
Inflation trends in UK	Production Schedules
Value Added Tax (VAT) rates	Office for National Statistics
Future production levels	Market Research
Demand for our products	SWOT analysis
	HMRC website
	Gross National Product
	New York Times

2.2   **(a)**   Which **one** of the following has an effect on the reliability of a forecast which has been based on sampling?

   (a)   The size of the sample

   (b)   Whether the sample was random or non-random

   (c)   The size of the population from which the sample was drawn

   (d)   Whether the sample was quasi-random or quota based

   (e)   All of the above

   (b)   Which **two** of the following constitute good guidelines for the use of price index numbers for budgeting?

   (a)   Use as general an index as possible

   (b)   Extrapolate past index numbers only when future prices are believed to follow past trends

   (c)   Choose index numbers that are as specific to the circumstances as possible

   (d)   Never attempt to use index numbers for budgeting prices

   (c)   At which stage in a product life cycle is trend analysis with seasonal variations likely to produce the best forecast? Select **one** answer.

   (a)   Start-up

   (b)   Growth

   (c)   Maturity

   (d)   Decline

2.3   An insurance company has analysed its sales of travel insurance over the last two years, and produced the following information:

Year	Quarter	Trend (Policies)	Seasonal Variation (Policies)
1	1	5,800	−430
	2	5,870	−350
	3	5,935	+880
	4	6,010	−100
2	1	6,090	−430
	2	6,165	−350
	3	6,220	+880
	4	6,290	−100

Required:

(a)   Calculate the average trend movement per quarter over the last two years.

(b)   Use the average trend movement to forecast the expected sales (in numbers of policies) in quarters 3 and 4 of year 3.

2.4   A computer program has used linear regression to analyse the sales data of Pegasus Limited, a garden ornament manufacturer. Using quarter numbers (quarter 1 is the first quarter of year 1) the sales trend has been determined as:

Sales Trend (in £) = (Quarter Number x £1,200) + £83,000.

The Seasonal Variations have been determined as the following percentages of the trend.

Quarter 1   −10%

Quarter 2   +80%

Quarter 3   +15%

Quarter 4   −85%

Required:

(a)   Use the above data to calculate the forecast of sales for Pegasus Limited in £ for each quarter of year 3.

(b)   Comment on any drawbacks of producing sales revenue forecasts directly in money amounts.

2.5 The data in the table below relates to numbers of attendances at a new minor injuries unit in a hospital. The unit operates a three shift system (morning, afternoon, and night). Each shift is treated as a seasonal variation.

Day	Shift	Attendances	Trend	Variations
1	Morning	75		
1	Afternoon	50		
1	Night	115		
2	Morning	90		
2	Afternoon	65		
2	Night	130		
3	Morning	105		
3	Afternoon	80		
3	Night	145		

Required:

(a) Complete the table using a 3 point moving average to identify the trend, and calculate the variations.

(b) Forecast the attendances in day 4 by extrapolating the data.

2.6 The trend for quarter 4 of the current year was sales of 220,000 units. The trend is increasing by 1% each quarter. Complete the table below to forecast the trend for each of the quarters of the coming year, and then adjust your figures for seasonal variations to give a forecast for actual sales. Do not show decimals; round your answers to the nearest whole number.

Next Year Sales Units	Quarter 1	Quarter 2	Quarter 3	Quarter 4
Trend				
Seasonal Variations	+10%	0	−15%	+5%
Forecast				

2.7   Forecasts are being prepared for three separate fixed costs, heating oil, electricity, and factory rent. The current costs are shown in the table below as 'year 0', and forecasts are required for next year (year 1) and the following year (year 2). The percentage increases or decreases shown relate to the anticipated change compared to the year immediately preceding the year being forecast.

Complete the table to show the forecast figures to the nearest £.

	Year 0 Costs £	Year 1 Changes	Year 1 Costs £	Year 2 Changes	Year 2 Costs £
Heating Oil	43,200	–8%		–2.5%	
Electricity	61,500	–1%		+3%	
Factory Rent	80,000	+2%		+2%	

2.8   Use the index numbers to adjust the prices shown in the table below. Give your answers rounded to the nearest penny.

	Material E	Material F	Material G	Material H
Current price	£18.00	£20.00	£65.00	£17.25
Current index	100	159	221	880
Forecast index	109	163	218	896
Forecast price				

3 Functional budgets

this chapter covers...

In this chapter we begin our examination of the preparation of budgets.

We start by learning the purposes of budgets, and see how some organisations view particular purposes as more important than others. We examine how budget setting links with the organisation's objectives and strategy, and must be built around the key (or principal) budget factor – which is often sales.

Next we examine the various budgets that are usually prepared, and how they are sequenced. The key budget factor is normally forecast first, and the other budgets are based around this important data.

We examine in detail how the budgets for a manufacturing organisation are prepared, including dealing with rejection rates, wastage and inefficiency.

Finally we discuss some techniques that can be applied to the construction of budgets for indirect costs and support functions.

THE PURPOSES OF BUDGETS

A budget is a financial plan for an organisation, prepared in advance.

In any organisation the budget provides the mechanism by which the objectives of the organisation can be achieved. In this way it forms a link between the current position and the position that the organisation's managers are aiming for. By using a budget firstly to plan and then to monitor, the managers can ensure that the organisation's progress is co-ordinated to achieve the objectives of the organisation. The specific purposes and benefits of using budgets are as follows.

1 the budget compels planning

By formalising the agreed objectives of the organisation through a budget preparation system, an organisation can ensure that its plans are achievable. It will be able to decide what resources are required to produce the desired outputs, and to make sure that they will be available at the right time.

2 the budget communicates and coordinates

Because a budget will be agreed by an organisation, all the relevant personnel will be working towards the same ends. During the budget setting process any anticipated problems should be resolved and any areas of potential confusion clarified. All the organisation's departments should be in a position to play their part in achieving the overall goals. This objective of all parts of the organisation working towards the same ends is sometimes referred to as '**goal congruence**'.

3 the budget can be used to authorise

For organisations where control of activities is deemed to be a high priority the budget can be used as the primary tool to ensure conformity to agreed plans. Once the budget is agreed it can effectively become the authority to follow a particular course of action or spend a certain amount of money. Public sector organisations, with their necessary emphasis on strict accountability, will tend to take this approach, as will some commercial organisations that choose not to delegate too much authority.

4 the budget can be used to monitor and control

An important reason for producing a budget is that management is able to monitor the actual results against the budget. This is so that action can be taken to modify the operation of the organisation as time passes, or possibly to change the budget if it becomes unachievable. This is similar to the way that standard costing is used to monitor and control costs, and can be used alongside that technique.

5 the budget can be used to motivate

A budget can be part of the organisation's techniques for motivating managers and other staff to achieve the organisation's objectives. The extent to which this happens will depend on how the budget is agreed and set, and whether it is perceived as fair and achievable. The budget may also be linked to rewards (for example bonuses) where targets are met or exceeded. We will examine how the way budgets are prepared can affect motivation in Chapter 6.

THE INITIAL STEPS IN BUDGET PREPARATION

the aims of an organisation

Before an organisation's managers can begin to build a useful budget there are several initial steps that must be taken. These are based around the fundamental questions about the **aims** – the 'vision' – of the organisation:

'where do we want it to go?' and

'how do we get it there?'

These are essentially long-term issues, and once agreed upon would not tend to be changed very often.

objectives and strategy

For a budget to be of use to an organisation it must be a mechanism of helping the organisation achieve its **objectives**. The objectives are the targets that the managers of the organisation wish it to achieve. The way in which these objectives are expressed will depend upon the type of organisation and the way in which it operates. For example a pet food manufacturer may have the specific objective of obtaining sales penetration of 25% of the UK dog food market, whereas an independent TV production company may have the objective of achieving a certain number of viewers on average.

The organisation must then develop a **strategy** for achieving those objectives. Several alternatives may need to be considered before the final strategy is decided upon. The pet food company mentioned in the above example may decide that it needs to develop and market a new food product for young dogs to help it to achieve its objective. The independent TV production company may have a strategy of producing pilots for ten new programmes each year from which it can then develop the most promising.

relevant data

Before any progress can be made in preparing a budget, relevant data must be identified and collected. We have already seen that information must be available about the aims, objectives and strategy of the organisation so that the budget that is prepared will be consistent with these. The following are examples of the types of data that can be used in developing the budget. The data is divided into data from internal and external sources.

data from internal sources

■ **accounting information**
This will include information about the accounting system (eg specific accounting polices) and how they will affect the budget, as well as data collected through the accounting system (for example historical costs).

■ **wage and salary information**
The resource of labour is clearly fundamental to many organisations, and sufficient information must be available to incorporate as appropriate.

data from external sources

■ **information about suppliers and availability of inputs**
Information must be available about suppliers' ability to supply the inputs required by the organisation, as well as data about relevant prices. This issue may be relevant to the consideration of limiting factors and can also force revisions to the budget as examined in Chapter 5.

■ **information about customers and markets**
It would not make sense to plan to make goods or provide services that were not required in the market place. Information of this type is fundamental to developing valid budgets.

■ **general economic information**
The impact of the economy on projections is discussed later in this chapter. No organisation can exist in a vacuum and those preparing budgets must recognise the importance of the health of the economy in which they operate.

Information from all these areas will be needed at various points in the budgeting process that is described in this chapter and the next.

limiting factors – the 'key' budget factor

When an organisation prepares a budget, it must first analyse its **limiting factors** – the issues that determine the level of its output. For a commercial organisation these could include:

- the size of its market
- capacity of its premises
- availability of raw material
- amount of working capital
- availability of skilled workers

One of the factors will be the main one that affects the activity level of the organisation – the **key budget factor**. This is the factor (sometimes known as the 'principal budget factor') that all the aspects of the operation depend upon. For most manufacturing or trading operations the key budget factor is **sales**; the assumptions that are made about the level of sales in the budget will affect all the other parts of the budget. This is because the organisation will plan to support the budgeted sales level and build the budgets and assumptions around this one factor.

Although sales level is the most common key factor, some commercial organisations may decide that a different factor is the most important in their particular circumstances. For example, if a manufacturer can sell all that it produces, but has production restricted by lack of skilled labour then the assumed labour level would become the key budget factor. A similar situation would arise if there were production restrictions caused by shortages of raw materials, or limited machine capacity.

Non-commercial organisations will also need to identify their key budget factor, and build their budgets around their assumptions concerning it. Charities and government agencies may consider that there is a demand for their services that is virtually limitless; their principal (key) budget factor is the amount of money they receive to fund what they do. For example, the Government's healthcare provision is limited by the amount of funding it can get from the government spending allocation and from private enterprise. The demand for Oxfam's aid is very high, but its key budget factor is the amount of money it can expect to raise to fund that aid.

There may be times when a limiting factor changes during a budget period as a result of changing demand or availability of resources. The issues of dealing with limited materials, labour and production capacity are examined in Chapter 5.

the initial budgeting process

If we combine the ideas just discussed then the initial budget process for an established organisation would follow the pattern in the diagram at the top of the next page.

the initial budgeting process

review the organisation's objectives

review the organisation's strategy for achieving its objectives

identify all of the organisation's current limiting factors

identify the key budget factor

forecast the level of this key factor

build the budgets around this forecast

CO-ORDINATING THE MAIN TYPES OF BUDGET

Once the key factor has been determined, and an appropriate forecast developed, the budgets for the whole organisation can be generated. For a manufacturing organisation these would typically include:

sales budget	usually generated directly from the key factor – the forecast data
production budget	based on the sales budget together with the anticipated finished goods inventory levels
materials usage budget	based on the production budget
materials purchase budget	based on the materials usage budget, together with the anticipated materials inventory levels
labour utilisation budget	also based on the production budget
functional budgets	to support the operation (often based on departments), for example administration budget, finance budget; these may not be so dependent upon the sales level as other budgets that are linked more closely
capital expenditure budget	this would also have to be developed in conjunction with the revenue budgets to ensure that the agreed spending on new or replacement equipment was in place

cash flow budget	this would take account of all the other budgets and their effect on the organisation's liquidity – note that this is not a functional budget, but is a part of the master budget
master budget	the calculations from all the revenue and capital budgets contribute to the **master budget** which takes the form of a budgeted statement of profit or loss and a budgeted statement of financial position together with a cash budget

The choice and format of the main budgets will need to be appropriate to the organisation. In Chapter 1 we examined responsibility accounting, and how responsibility centres can be used. Appropriate cost centres, profit centres and investment centres will need to be defined, and the budgets will need to be structured accordingly. For example, if there are separate cost centres for 'administration' and 'marketing' then there needs to be administration and marketing budgets. In this way managers can be held to account for their department's performance.

the effect of changing inventory levels

You will have noticed several references in the list of budgets to **inventory levels**. Where inventory levels are to remain constant the situation is simple. For example the production budget will be identical to the sales budget if the finished goods inventory level is to remain unchanged, ie the amount you will produce will be the amount you estimate you are going to sell. However if the inventory level is to increase then the extra units of goods that will go into inventory will need to be produced in addition to the units that are to be sold in the budget period. This is a concept that we will return to frequently.

CREATING BUDGETS

Earlier in this chapter we examined the methods and implications of creating budgets and using budgetary control. We will now look at the numerical work that is needed to produce a budget. This will involve co-ordinating the various budgets so that they are all based on the same assumptions and fit together in a logical sequence. In any tasks involving the preparation of budgets, you may be requested to state the assumptions that they are based on.

The procedure that we will need to follow when creating budgets is based on the system described in the earlier section on coordinated budgets. Limiting factors need to be considered and the 'key' factor identified. For a manufacturing business sales volume is often the principal (key) budget factor. The system of budgets that will be created is shown in the diagram below and explained in the text that follows. The diagram also shows how the relevant budgets link with the cash budget.

sales budget

The forecast of sales units will need to be developed first, as this is fundamental to the whole series of budgets. The level of actual production that is required will depend on two issues:

- the amount of finished goods the business plans to hold in stock ready to be sold (inventory)
- whether any of the finished goods are likely to be rejected

sales revenue budget

The sales budget in units can be used to develop the sales revenue budget. This uses the sales units multiplied by the unit selling prices to arrive at the budgeted sales revenue. This budget will ultimately be used to develop the budgeted statement of profit or loss. The data from the sales revenue budget will also link with the cash budget, which will use information on the timing of the receipts.

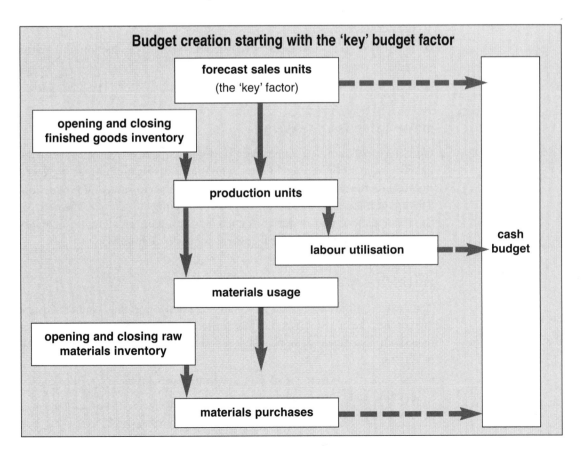

production budget

We will generally need to plan to produce the units that we intend to sell, but we can

- plan to reduce our production by the intended fall in the level of finished goods inventory, or

- plan to increase our production to increase the level of our finished goods inventory

The production budget in units for a period therefore equals:

Budgeted Sales Units

– Opening Inventory of Finished Goods

+ Closing Inventory of Finished Goods

This can be justified since:

- the **opening inventory** of finished goods has already been produced, and can therefore be deducted from our calculation of what needs to be made, and

- the **closing inventory** has yet to be made so needs to be added in to our total of goods to be produced

In summary, the common-sense rule is:

- if inventory of finished goods is to increase, then production must be greater than sales

- if finished goods inventory is to remain constant, production will be the same as sales

- if finished goods inventory is to fall, production will be less than sales

materials usage budget

Once the production budget has been developed in units, we can calculate the quantity of material we need to use. The **materials usage budget** is created to ascertain the amount of raw material that will be consumed in production. The use of materials can also be valued at this point if required. The data for these calculations may come from standard costing information, or some less formal estimates of the material content of production units.

materials purchases budget

The materials purchases budget can be created once the materials usage budget has been established. Here differences between the quantity of material to be consumed in production and the quantity to be purchased will be due to:

- the required movement in raw material goods inventory (adjusting for opening and closing inventory)

- any wastage or loss of raw materials

We will examine how to account for wastage later in this chapter. At this point we will consider the adjustments needed for raw material inventory movements.

The reasoning follows a similar pattern to the one described for sales, finished goods and production. If we already have raw materials in the opening inventory this amount does not have to be purchased, but the quantity that we plan to have remaining at the end of the period must be purchased in addition to the amount that will be used in production.

The **quantity of material purchased** (as recorded in the material purchases budget) will therefore equal:

Quantity of material to be used (per materials usage budget)

– opening inventory of raw materials,

+ closing inventory of raw materials.

The rule is therefore:

▪ if inventory of raw materials is to increase, then purchases must be greater than materials usage

▪ if raw materials inventory is to remain constant, then purchases will be the same as materials usage

▪ if raw materials inventory is to fall, then purchases will be less than materials usage

One vital reason for creating a material purchases budget is that the information on the timing of purchases will feed into the cash budget which shows when the payments will need to be made.

Case Study	# FLUMEN LIMITED: # BUDGETS FOR MATERIALS USED AND PURCHASED

situation

A manufacturing company, Flumen Limited, makes a single product, the Wye. The sales forecast for February is 5,900 units. Each unit of Wye uses 5 kilos of Monnow and 3 kilos of Lugg.

The anticipated inventory levels at the beginning of February are:

Finished Wyes	1,400 units
Unused Monnow	350 kilos
Unused Lugg	200 kilos

The required inventory levels at the end of February are:

Finished Wyes	1,800 units
Unused Monnow	250 kilos
Unused Lugg	450 kilos

required

Produce the following budget figures for the month of February:

(a)   Production of Wye (in units)

(b)   Materials usage of Monnow and Lugg (in kilos)

(c)   Materials purchases of Monnow and Lugg (in kilos)

solution

(a)   Production units =

Budgeted Sales Units	5,900
– opening Inventory of finished goods	(1,400)
+ closing Inventory of finished goods	1,800
Production units =	6,300

                                                                        Wyes

(b)   Materials usage

Monnow: 6,300 x 5 kilos = 31,500 kilos

Lugg: 6,300 x 3 kilos = 18,900 kilos

(c)   Materials purchases:

Monnow:

Quantity of material to be used	31,500 kilos
– opening inventory of raw materials	(350 kilos)
+ closing inventory of raw materials	250 kilos
Required purchases of Monnow	31,400 kilos

Lugg:

Quantity of material to be used	18,900 kilos
– opening inventory of raw materials	(200 kilos)
+ closing inventory of raw materials	450 kilos
Required purchases of Lugg	19,150 kilos

labour utilisation budget

This budget (also known as the direct labour budget) is developed based on the production requirements (in units) shown in the production budget. The labour utilisation budget is usually based on direct labour time in hours, but could be converted into full time equivalent employees.

At this point it will be determined whether there are sufficient basic labour hours available for the production requirements, or whether overtime will need to be worked. Sometimes the amount of labour time available is a limiting factor (as discussed earlier) and it may be that sub-contractors can be used to make up any shortfall. This is an example of the benefits of good budgeting – so that the labour resources can be planned to ensure that production can go ahead as required.

worked example – calculating overtime hours

During week 50, the production budget shows a requirement for manufacturing 12,083 units. Each unit takes 11 minutes of direct labour time. There are 52 direct labour employees, each working 38 hours per week. Overtime hours can be worked if necessary.

Calculate the overtime requirement, rounded up to the next whole hour.

Direct labour hours needed:

> 12,083 units x 11 minutes / 60 = 2,216 hours (rounded up)

Basic rate hours available:

> 52 employees x 38 hours =1,976 hours

Overtime hours required:

> 2,216 hours – 1,976 hours = 240 hours

worked example – calculating sub-contracting work

During week 51, the production budget shows a requirement for manufacturing 14,180 units. Each unit takes 11 minutes of direct labour time. There are 52 direct labour employees, each working 38 hours per week. Overtime hours can be worked if necessary, but only up to an average of 8 hours per employee. Production requirements in excess of those that can be carried out by employees must be sub-contracted to another company.

Calculate how many units can be made in-house (rounded down) and how many must be sub-contracted (rounded up to the next whole unit).

Total number of units to be produced: = 14,180 units

Maximum number of units to be made in-house:

(52 employees x (38 + 8) hours) / (11 minutes / 60)   = 13,047 units (rounded down)

Number of units to be sub-contracted:

14,180 – 13,047.27   = 1,133 units (rounded up)

Note the way that the rounding is carried out in this example. It would not make sense to only make a part of a unit in-house. All units made must add up to the total requirement.

Once the direct labour requirement has been established, then costs can be calculated based on known basic labour and overtime rates. Where sub-contracting is also needed then these costs can be determined based on relevant quotations or estimates.

Indirect costs in the form of fixed and variable overheads can also be ascertained at this stage if required. If absorption costing is being used then the overheads may be absorbed using a direct labour hour rate. If marginal costing is adopted all fixed costs will be considered as relating to the time period rather than the production units.

machine utilisation budget

Another useful budget that can be prepared once the production budget has been finalised is the machine utilisation budget. This shows the extent to which existing production machines are used for the planned production level, and also provides an opportunity to plan for short-term hire of additional machines.

worked example – calculating machine utilisation

During week 52, the production budget shows a requirement for manufacturing 10,120 units. The company owns twelve machines, each one is capable of producing up to 1,125 units per week.

Calculate the machine utilisation percentage (to the nearest whole percentage), and state whether all twelve machines are needed in week 52.

The maximum total machine capacity is 12 x 1,125 = 13,500 units

$$\text{Machine utilisation} = \frac{\text{production requirement}}{\text{maximum total machine capacity}} \times 100$$

$$= \frac{10,120}{13,500} \times 100 = 75\% \text{ (rounded)}$$

The unused capacity is (13,500 – 10,120) = 3,380 units. This is just over the capacity of three machines, so three machines are not needed at all during week 52.

If this production level was expected to continue for the foreseeable future, then consideration could be given to selling or scrapping up to three machines. However, care would have to be taken to avoid leaving the organisation with a problem should production levels rise.

Based on the current twelve machines, if the production budget had a requirement for more than 13,500 units, then additional machines may need to be hired. This is provided, of course, that there is sufficient direct labour for the expected production level.

REJECTS, WASTAGE AND INEFFICIENCY

the problems

The range of problems that we must be able to deal with include:

■ **producing finished goods that are not up to standard**

Depending on the production process and the quality control system, some finished goods that are not up to standard may be only detected once they have been manufactured. This means that we must plan to produce more than we need so that the expected number of rejects is allowed for. An example of the type of product where rejection may occur after completion is electronic components that would undergo a final quality test.

■ **wastage of raw materials**

In some situations the amount of raw materials that is contained in the finished product may be less than the amount that must be purchased. This can be due to a variety of situations occurring before or during manufacture, including deterioration, spillage, or evaporation. It can also occur due to the raw materials naturally including unusable parts. An example of this could be timber that needs to have the bark removed before being cut to size.

■ **a labour force that is not operating at 100% efficiency**

When standard efficiency levels are used to plan for the amount of direct labour time to produce the required output, problems will arise if the workforce is significantly slower (or faster) than expected. When this difference can be anticipated the budgets can be modified to take account of the different efficiency level. This could occur (for example) if a workforce was undergoing training to use new equipment.

how to deal with the problems

The issues that we face when preparing budgets incorporating these situations are:

■ In which budget should we account for the situation?

■ How do we accurately account for the situation?

The diagram on the next page summarises the first of these issues. It is based on the budget preparation diagram shown earlier in this chapter.

The problems described earlier are dealt with at the following points in the overall budgeting process:

■ anticipated **rejections** of finished goods are built into the **production budget**. We therefore plan to produce enough so that when some output has been scrapped there is still enough to sell and account for changes in finished goods inventory levels

■ **wastage of materials during production** is accounted for when determining the **materials usage budget**. A higher level of usage is planned for so that the materials will still be sufficient, despite wastage during production

■ **wastage of materials before the production process** commences is taken account of when the **materials purchases budget** is prepared. In this way sufficient materials are acquired to deal with wastage, the amount needed for the materials usage budget, and the required changes in raw materials inventory levels

■ **non-productive time** is built into the **labour utilisation budget**. We plan for sufficient time to be available so that the productive part is enough to satisfy the needs of the production budget

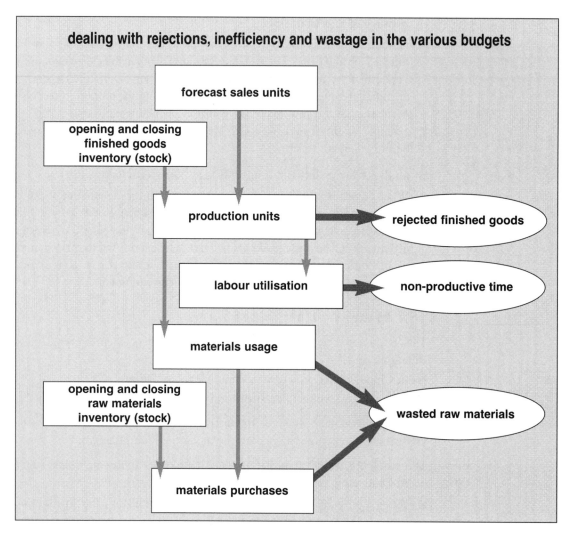

dealing with rejections, inefficiency and wastage in the various budgets

REJECTION OF FINISHED GOODS

The approach to take when dealing with a situation where finished goods are scrapped after a final inspection is to work back from the number of perfect products that we need to make. This is illustrated in the following Case Study.

Case Study

OSBORNE ELECTRICAL COMPONENTS: REJECTION OF FINISHED GOODS

An electrical component manufacturer's system involves a quality control check of all the completed components. The records show that on average 6% of completed components will fail this check and will need to be scrapped.

The forecast sales volume for the month of March is 5,200 components, and the production budget is to incorporate an increase in finished goods inventory from 1,000 components to 1,440 components, as well as the typical failure rate.

required

Calculate the production budget (in numbers of components) for March.

solution

Both the sales forecast and the finished goods inventory increase must be based on 'good' components. It would not make sense to sell or place into inventory any units that had failed the quality inspection.

The number of 'good' components required is therefore:

Budgeted Sales Units	5,200
– opening Inventory of Finished Goods	(1,000)
+ closing Inventory of Finished Goods	1,440
= production of 'good' components	5,640

But actual production must be greater than this amount to account for rejects. Since the rejection rate is assumed to be 6%, the 5,640 'good' units must equal 94% of the required production level, as demonstrated in this diagram.

reject units	6% of production
'good' units (5,640)	94% of production

The production budget must therefore equal 5,640 x 100 ÷ 94 = 6,000 units.

You should be careful to note that the calculation does not involve simply adding 6% to the good production, but is effectively adding 6/94, because the good production is 94% of the total production. This technique is often examined, and is a frequent source of confusion amongst students.

Note that you can always check your answer. If 6% of 6,000 units are rejected, ie 360 are rejected, 5,640 units are left.

MATERIAL WASTAGE DURING PRODUCTION

Wastage during manufacture is a common problem, and occurs in industries as diverse as food production and house building. There can also be situations where one material incurs wastage, while another adds to the weight of the finished product. The next Case Study examines this problem.

COOL CHIP COMPANY: MATERIAL WASTAGE

A frozen potato chip manufacturer purchases whole potatoes with skins. These are then peeled, any imperfections are removed, and the potatoes are sliced into chips and fried before freezing. The average wastage that occurs during peeling and imperfection removal is 20% of the weight of the whole potatoes.

No further wastage occurs during slicing, or frying.

The production budget for July is for 100,000 kilos of frozen chips, based on their weight immediately prior to freezing.

required

Calculate the materials usage budget (in kilos) for July for whole raw potatoes.

solution

In order to calculate the usage we must work back from the production budget:

To produce 100,000 kilos of uncooked chips we need to start with a larger weight of whole potatoes. The uncooked chips represent 80% of the weight of the whole potatoes, since 20% is lost as skin and imperfections.

Therefore whole potatoes will equal 100,000 x 100 ÷ 80 = 125,000 kilos.

The materials utilisation budget will therefore be:

125,000 kilos whole potatoes.

It is worth double-checking our calculation. This can be done as follows:

125,000 kilos whole potatoes used, less 20% wastage at the peeling stage, leaving 100,000 (80%) chips.

MATERIAL WASTAGE BEFORE PRODUCTION

The final type of situation that you may need to deal with involves wastage occurring while the material is being stored, prior to production. In the next Case Study this idea has been combined with the technique from the last Case Study to show how to deal with wastage when it occurs at two points; one before production starts and the other during production.

Case Study

WALVERN WATER LIMITED: MATERIAL WASTAGE

A manufacturer uses large quantities of distilled water in its production process. It buys the water in bulk and keeps it in large storage tanks. Due to the temperature in the vicinity of the factory, it is estimated that 3% of the distilled water will have evaporated between being purchased and being drawn from the storage tanks. A further 5% of the distilled water that is used in the process evaporates during production.

The final product has a distilled water content that is 89% of its volume.

The production budget for June shows that 390,000 litres of the finished product is required.

The distilled water inventory is estimated at 50,000 litres at the start of June, and 80,000 litres at the end of June (both figures assume that the initial evaporation in storage has taken place).

required

Calculate the following data for the distilled water for June:

1   the volume to be input into the production process, and

2   the volume to be purchased

Carry out calculations to the nearest litre.

solution

As in the other case studies, we need to work back from the required output.

1   The finished goods will contain (390,000 litres x 89%) = 347,100 litres of distilled water.

   Evaporation during the production process means that this figure is equal to 95% of the distilled water input into the process.

   The volume to be input is therefore (347,100 x 100 ÷ 95) = 365,368 litres.

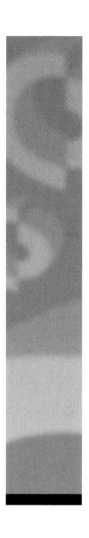

2   We therefore need to purchase sufficient distilled water to allow for:

the evaporation in storage, *plus*

the required increase in distilled water inventory, *plus*

the volume to be input into the production process.

The following diagram illustrates the amount of water that will need to be purchased:

evaporation during storage
increase in inventory level
input into production

As calculated in part 1, 365,368 litres needs to be input into production. A further 30,000 litres are needed to increase the inventory level (from 50,000 litres to 80,000 litres).

This means that (365,368 + 30,000) = 395,368 litres are needed after evaporation in storage.

Since the evaporation in storage is estimated at 3% of the amount initially acquired, the above amount that we need must represent 97% of the amount that we must purchase.

We therefore need to purchase (395,368 x 100 ÷ 97) = 407,596 litres

LABOUR EFFICIENCY

When a lack of efficiency results in non-productive time, the problem should be dealt with at the time the labour utilisation budget is being drawn up. By definition, non-productive time cannot be used to produce output, and so the amount of time that can be effectively used in production is less than the time that must be allowed for in total (and paid for).

If, on the other hand, it is anticipated that the efficiency level will be more than 100% (ie the work is to be carried out more quickly than the standard) this would also be accounted for at the same point in the process.

These two possibilities – inefficiency and a high level of efficiency – are dealt with in the Case Studies that follow.

PERFECT PATIOS:
LOW LABOUR EFFICIENCY

A company that manufactures paving slabs has traditionally used standard labour times to build up the labour utilisation budget. Output is measured in hundreds of slabs, and the standard direct labour time to manufacture 100 type A slabs is 3.6 hours, and 100 type B slabs is 4.2 hours.

Recent legislation means that additional break times need to be accounted for in the labour utilisation budget. It is estimated that break times will in future account for 12% of the direct labour time allocated to production work, This has not been accounted for in the standard times quoted.

The production budget for January is for 24,000 type A slabs and 58,000 type B slabs.

required

Calculate the labour utilisation budget (in total direct labour hours) for January.

solution

The productive time (excluding breaks) is as follows:

Type A slabs:
     240 (hundreds of slabs) x 3.6 hours   =   864 hours
Type B slabs:
     580 (hundreds of slabs) x 4.2 hours   =   2,436 hours

Total productive time   3,300 hours

This productive time will equal 88% of the total paid time due to the 12% allowance for breaks, as shown here.

break times	12%
productive time (3,300 hours)	88%

The total paid time will therefore equal 3,300 hours x 100 ÷ 88 = 3,750 hours, and 3,750 direct labour hours will form the labour utilisation budget.

**Case
Study**

SLICK PERFORMERS LTD:
HIGH LABOUR EFFICIENCY

A small pottery that makes rustic crockery by hand set its standards some time ago, when the potters were relatively inexperienced. These standards included a time of 8 hours to create a 48-piece dinner service using a potter's wheel. Since that time all the potters have become more proficient, and can now produce work of the same standard more quickly. It is estimated that they are currently working at a 120% efficiency level based on the old standards. During the coming month of April the pottery needs to fulfil orders for 32 dinner services, and also increase its inventory level from 3 dinner services to 7 dinner services.

required

Calculate the labour utilisation budget for creating dinner services (in total direct labour hours) for April.

solution

The production required for April will be:

32	dinner services (for current orders), *plus*
4	dinner services (for increase in inventory)
$\overline{36}$	dinner services

At the standard time of 8 hours per dinner service, this would take 288 standard hours. Since the potters are working at 120% efficiency they will take less time than standard. This is calculated as:

288 hours x 100 ÷ 120 = <u>240 hours</u>

The logic can be checked by working back from the solution as follows:

At the standard rate (of 8 hours per set) in 240 hours they could make
240 ÷ 8 = 30 dinner services

Operating at 120% efficiency they can produce 20% more output, ie
30 x 120% = 36 dinner services

BUDGETING FOR INDIRECT COSTS AND SUPPORT ACTIVITIES

We discussed in Chapter 1 how budgets are used based on responsibility accounting. Separate budgets will be prepared for each function of the organisation (divided up if appropriate) and individual managers will be held accountable for their department's performance against their budget. As we move away from budgets for the production department into the budgets which manage indirect costs in the various support functions (for example distribution, marketing, administration and finance), there are a number of different approaches that could be used. The indirect costs in these functions will typically not vary directly with production output, and so can be budgeted for in ways that best suit the organisation.

The following alternative approaches can be taken to preparing these functional budgets.

incremental budgeting

Preparing budgets using incremental budgeting is the traditional approach. It involves basing the budget for a period on the previous period's budget (or actual costs), and then making adjustments for anticipated inflation and any other expected changes. In this way, incremental budgeting produces a series of budgets over time that change only gradually. This provides consistency and security within the departments, and can avoid conflict between departments as resources are allocated based on agreed principles.

There are, however, disadvantages to incremental budgeting:

■ there are no incentives for developing new ideas, or reducing costs. Managers may feel that they must spend all their budget to avoid it being reduced in future

■ over time the budgets may become out of line with the amount of work carried out in the department, or the usefulness of that work

■ if the departmental managers build in some 'budgetary slack' – by obtaining a larger budget than is really needed – then this may go unchallenged for many years

zero based budgeting (ZBB)

This method of budgeting takes the opposite approach to incremental budgeting. In each period the budget starts from a base of zero, with no account taken of the previous period's budget. Each cost that is agreed for the department has to be justified based on the benefit that will arise to the organisation from spending the amount allocated.

Often alternative 'decision packages' are prepared for the department showing the costs that would be incurred to deliver certain levels of benefits. For example, alternative decision packages for a credit control section could involve:

■ an option of a high level of interaction with debtors including active management of credit limits and a variety of appropriate actions on outstanding amounts to provide maximum receipts. This package would be labour intensive and expensive

■ an option involving a lower level of interaction with debtors, with fewer options to use to chase outstanding amounts. The receipts would flow into the organisation more slowly and bad debts may increase, but the cost of running the department would be much less than the first option

The costs and benefits of providing each level of service would need to be analysed and a decision made based on the outcome that was best for achieving the organisational objectives.

The following are some advantages of zero based budgeting:

■ it forces re-evaluation of the activities within each function, and how they contribute to achieving the organisation's objectives

■ it encourages innovation and links the uses of resources to the achievement of results

■ it avoids wastage and budgetary slack

However, there are some disadvantages:

■ the process is very time-consuming and expensive to operate

■ it may focus on short-term benefits at the expense of the long term (for example when applied to training or marketing)

■ the judging of decision packages may be difficult and subjective

One approach that could be taken is to rotate the use of zero based budgeting so that each budget centre does not go through the process each year. For example, a department may undertake a full zero based exercise once every five years, with incremental budgeting used in the other years. This would reduce the cost, but retain some of the benefits.

priority based budgeting

Priority based budgeting shares some of its ideas with zero based budgeting in that it can ignore previous budgets. It examines the outcomes that an organisation is attempting to achieve and prioritises them – allocating resources to the outcomes that are judged to be most important. It is a technique that is frequently used in the public sector where diverse services compete for limited resources, for example local authorities and police forces. It is especially useful for situations where resources are being reduced, and provides some rigour for making tough decisions.

Where appropriate, it can use input from the service users as well as the organisation managers. For example, views about the relative priority that should be given to public library services, rubbish collection, and street lighting could be sought from the public in a local area.

Some organisations use a scale (for example 10 points) to link to each element of a service provided ranging from 'critical' (must be funded)

through 'desirable' (may be funded) to services that are unjustifiable. The resources are then applied to programmes or services working down the list from the most important until the budgeted resources are used up.

activity based budgeting (ABB)

Unlike the three approaches to budgeting that we have just discussed, activity based budgeting is often used to manage indirect costs **within** the production department. In Chapter 1 we discussed how activity based costing could be used to allocate costs in the most appropriate way based on how activities use resources. Activity based budgeting links with ABC to provide a system that uses the same mechanism to budget as is used to develop costs.

Activity based budgeting uses the same cost drivers that were identified through ABC. The budgeting follows three stages:

- activities and their cost drivers are first identified
- the number of units of cost driver that are required to complete the required activity level is then forecast
- the budgeted 'cost driver rate' can then be used

For example, suppose the production department was planning to manufacture 5,000 units of a particular product using 10 batches of 500 units each. As each batch required one set-up (the cost driver) of the production machinery, the cost of 10 'set-ups' would be budgeted for. This would be a more precise way of budgeting than just considering set-up costs as part of general production overheads.

It would make sense to use activity based budgeting in conjunction with activity based costing.

Chapter Summary

■ Budgets can be used to compel planning, to communicate and coordinate ideas, and to monitor and control outcomes. They may also be used to help motivate managers and employees.

■ Budgets must be in line with the objectives of the organisation, and the organisation's chosen strategy to achieve those objectives. Before starting to create a budget, the key budget factor must be recognised, and its numerical impact forecast. For most commercial organisations this factor is the sales level, but it could be based on specific resources or factors.

■ Budgets that are prepared for manufacturing organisations typically include Sales, Production, Materials Usage, Materials Purchases, and Labour Utilisation, together with other budgets including various functional (including departmental) budgets, capital expenditure budgets and cash budgets. These are coordinated and amalgamated to form a set of Master Budgets.

■ When preparing budgets we must accurately account for rejection of finished goods, a labour force that is not operating at 100% efficiency, or wastage of materials that occurs during or before production. In each situation care must be taken to allow for the correct quantity of unusable resources.

■ The expected level of rejection of finished goods that are not up to standard is allowed for when the production budget is prepared. An additional amount of production is planned so that once goods have been scrapped there is still sufficient to sell and place in inventory.

■ Any expected over or under efficiency of the direct labour force is built into the labour utilisation budget so that the amount of productive working will be sufficient to meet the needs of the production budget.

■ Planned wastage of raw materials during production is built into the materials utilisation budget. In this way the plan is modified to input additional materials to allow for the situation. Where the wastage is expected to occur before production, the materials purchases budget must be modified so that there will be enough materials to be used in production, once wastage and inventory movements have taken place.

■ A range of techniques can be used to help create ongoing budgets for indirect costs and support activities. These include the traditional incremental budgeting as well as the more recent developments of zero based budgeting, priority based budgeting and activity based budgeting.

budget	a financial plan for an organisation, prepared before the period starts
key budget factor	the main factor (internal or external) that determines the planned activity level of the organisation
production budget	a budget that plans how much should be produced in a particular period, to allow for anticipated sales, inventory movements of finished goods, and rejections due to poor quality
labour utilisation budget	a budget that details the labour input required to meet the needs of the production budget
materials usage budget	a budget that plans the amount of materials that is required to satisfy the production budget, after allowing for wastage during production
materials purchases budget	a budget that plans for the level of purchases needed to meet the demands of the materials utilisation budget, as well as allowing for wastage before production and changing inventory levels
machine utilisation budget	a budget that shows the extent to which owned or rented machinery will be utilised by production
incremental budgeting	preparing a budget by basing it on the budget for the previous period with adjustments for inflation and known changes
zero based budgeting	preparing a budget without reference to the previous period, but by analysing the costs and benefits of a series of decision packages
priority based budgeting	ranking outcomes into levels of priority as a means of budgeting only for those with the highest priorities
activity based budgeting	using the techniques of activity based costing to prepare budgets based on activities and their cost drivers

Activities

3.1 Suggest the key (or principal) budget factors for the following organisations:

(a) A partnership of two craftsmen who make high quality violins for leading musicians. The work is labour intensive and highly skilled. They are able to easily sell all they produce.

(b) A transport company that has a contract to work only for a major supplier of turkeys. The turkey supplier is currently expanding, but there is an agreement in place for all their transport requirements to be met by this one company for the next 12 months.

(c) A company whose team of engineers has a contract to maintain the Metro in Manchester. They have no plans to seek other contracts.

(d) A company that has opened a new baked potato outlet on a busy business park. The firm has the sole rights to supply potatoes to the 3,000 staff on the site, and has the capacity to cook and sell 100 baked potatoes per day.

3.2 The following table shows the sales level in units planned for the next three months. The company policy is to hold inventory of finished goods at the end of each month equal to 20% of the next month's sales.

Period	October	November	December
Sales (units)	20,400	21,600	24,000
Opening inventory	4,080		
Closing inventory			
Production (units)			

Complete the table to show the opening and closing inventory and production in units for October and November.

3.3 A manufacturing company that makes kitchen chairs is planning its activities for month 5 in the current year. The following data is available:

Sales in month 5 are forecast at 1,800 units.

Each completed unit requires 4 kilos of raw material.

Planned inventory levels are:

	Raw Materials	Finished Goods
At end of month 4	1,200 kilos	500 units
At end of month 5	1,500 kilos	400 units

Required:

Calculate the following budgets for month 5:

- production budget (in units)
- raw materials usage (in kilos)
- raw materials purchases (in kilos)

3.4 During month 4, the production budget shows a requirement for manufacturing 25,430 units. Each unit takes 9 minutes of direct labour time. There are 22 direct labour employees, each working 160 basic hours per month. Overtime hours can be worked if necessary.

Calculate the overtime requirement for month 4, rounded up to the next whole hour.

3.5 Labour hours:

- 72,000 units of product M are to be manufactured in May.
- Each one takes 5 minutes to produce.
- 30 staff will each work 180 hours basic time.

How many overtime hours must be worked to complete the production?

Select from:

(a) 360	
(b) 600	
(c) 720	
(d) 5,400	
(e) 6,000	

3.6 During month 5, the production budget shows a requirement for manufacturing 27,365 units. Each unit takes 9 minutes of direct labour time. There are 22 direct labour employees, each working 160 hours per month. Overtime hours can be worked if necessary, but only up to an average 20 hours per employee. Production requirements in excess of those that can be carried out by employees must be sub-contracted to another company.

Calculate how many units can be made in-house (rounded down if necessary) and how many must be sub-contracted.

3.7 Department Y manufactures three products, A, B and C.

(a) Calculate the machine hours required to manufacture these in November, using the following table.

Product	Units	Hours per unit	Hours required
A	240	1.5	
B	210	2.0	
C	170	3.0	
Total hours for department Y			

(b) There are three machines in the department.

Each machine can be used for 300 hours in November. Additional machines can be hired if required.

Calculate how many additional machines should be hired.

3.8 A company that manufactures a single product (the Zapp) is planning for the next six months. Each unit of Zapp produced uses 2 litres of Woo and 3 litres of Koo.

Each unit of Zapp takes 0.5 hours of direct labour to produce.

The anticipated demand for Zapp is as follows:

January	5,000	units
February	4,000	units
March	6,500	units
April	5,000	units
May	6,500	units
June	5,000	units

after which the demand can be assumed to stabilise at 5,000 units per month.

It will be company policy to maintain raw material inventory at a level of 100% of the following month's usage, and to maintain finished goods inventory at a level to satisfy half of the following month's estimated sales. Inventory held on 31 December was 3,000 finished Zapps, and 8,000 litres of Woo and 16,000 litres of Koo.

Required:

Calculate the following budgets for each month and in total:

- Production of Zapps (in units)

- Materials Usage (in litres of Woo and Koo)

- Materials Purchase (in litres of Woo and Koo)

- Direct Labour (in hours)

3.9 State which budget should be used to take account of each of the following anticipated situations:

(a) Reduction in finished goods inventory.

(b) Deterioration of raw materials whilst in storage.

(c) Rejection of finished goods at final inspection.

(d) Spillage of raw materials during production.

(e) Direct Labour working at 80% standard efficiency level.

(f) Increased demand for finished goods.

(g) Increase in raw material inventory.

3.10 The quarterly production requirements for product M are shown below.

10% of production fails the quality checks and must be scrapped.

How many items of product M must be manufactured to allow for waste?

	Month 1	Month 2	Month 3
Required units	144,000	180,000	162,000
Manufactured units			

3.11 The sales budget for A B Wainwright Limited's product is 13,000 units in April, 15,000 units in May, and 20,000 units in June. The company policy is to plan for month end finished goods inventory of half of the following month's sales demand. All goods are inspected upon completion, and at this point an estimated 12.5% of finished goods are scrapped due to faults.

Required:

Calculate the production budget for May in numbers of units.

3.12 The following table (in units) shows the sales level planned for the next three months. The company policy is to hold inventory of finished goods at the end of each month equal to 15% of the next month's sales. 4% of completed production is expected to fail a quality check and be rejected.

Period	January	February	March
Sales	61,200	64,800	63,000
Opening inventory	9,180		
Closing inventory			
Good Production			
Rejects			
Total Production			

Complete the table to show all the relevant figures for January and February. Round up the figures for rejects and total production if necessary.

3.13 The Super Soup Company needs 50 kg of prepared carrots as an ingredient in a one tonne batch of soup. During preparation 20% of the weight of the raw unprepared carrots is lost in peel and imperfections. What should the unprepared carrots utilisation budget be (in kilos) for week 15, when 30 tonnes of soup are to be made?

(a) 7,500 kg	
(b) 1,800 kg	
(c) 1,875 kg	
(d) 1,200 kg	

3.14   Raw Material purchases:

- 30,000 items of product N are to be manufactured in April.

- Each requires 1.5 metres of raw material.

- 10% of raw material is wasted during manufacture.

- The opening inventory of raw materials will be 24,000 metres.

- The closing inventory of raw materials will be 20,000 metres.

How much material must be purchased?

Select from:

(a) 18,000m	
(b) 26,222m	
(c) 45,500m	
(d) 46,000m	
(e) 54,000m	

4 **Master budgets**

this chapter covers...

We start this chapter with an examination of the organisation of the budgeting process. This includes explanations of the roles of the budget committee and the budget accountant as well as an overview of the likely timescales for budget preparation. The importance of honesty, openness and transparency in the budgeting process is emphasised.

The chapter then turns to the production of master budgets, and illustrates how various budgets are brought together to create an operating budget. Cash budget creation is also examined, including how lagging impacts on cash budgets and other relationships between accruals and cash budgeting.

We then briefly consider the implications of performance measurement to the creation of budgets, so that the same measures can be applied to both the budget data and, later on, the actual performance.

The chapter concludes with a discussion and illustration of the submission of budgets to the budget committee.

ORGANISATION OF THE BUDGETING PROCESS

the budget manual

For most organisations budget setting forms a vital part of the formal procedures: the organisation's method of budgeting will be set out in writing in its policy documents. These will include details of responsibilities and timetables. They may be combined into a **budget manual**.

The budget manual can be used to explain the 'why?' and the 'how?' of the organisation's approach to using budgets. It may include the following:

- the primary purposes of budgets for the organisation
- the types of budget that are to be produced
- what format is to be used for budgets
- how far in advance budgets are to be set
- who has responsibility for setting budgets
- who has responsibility for monitoring performance against budgets
- how often performance is to be monitored against budgets
- who has the authority to modify agreed budgets

the budget committee

The budget procedures may be the responsibility of a budget committee, chaired by the Managing Director or a person he/she has appointed. The composition of the committee may be set out in the budget manual, together with the committee's responsibilities. The budget committee may have the authority to modify the budget manual.

The committee will consist of senior representatives from all the departments, so that there is full communication and co-ordination throughout the organisation. In this way there should be full understanding about the overall objectives of the organisation, and the part that each department must play in the total picture. It would not make sense for the marketing department to plan a promotion of a product that the production department could not supply in sufficient quantities. This concept of everyone working towards the same result is referred to as 'goal congruence'.

It is important that all budget proposals are agreed with the budget holders, and because of the way it is comprised, the budget committee is an ideal mechanism for ensuring that this happens. Without agreement a budget is unlikely to form an effective tool. There must be opportunities at both the forecasting stage and the budgeting stage for relevant individuals to raise any queries and seek clarification of the data. Only by this process will all budget holders feel that they fully understand the budgets and the forecasts on which they are built.

The committee will not only set and agree the budget, but it will also be responsible for monitoring the budget once it is in place. For example they may wish to monitor on a quarterly, monthly, or weekly basis, and will also want to decide on how quickly the information should be available and in what format.

It is important that the information produced in both the original budget and the subsequent monitoring reports is in a form that satisfies the needs of budget holders. The majority of the budget holders will not have accounting backgrounds, and the budget committee must carefully choose formats so that all users can understand and make full use of the documents.

In organisations where there is no formal budget committee, alternative ways must be used to ensure that budgets are fully agreed and coordinated, and that they are presented in a form that meet the needs of budget holders. In small organisations this responsibility may fall to the person who fulfils the role of management accountant, so they must be careful to carry out these duties effectively.

budget accountant

The budget accountant has a key role in the budgeting process within an organisation. Although the duties and responsibilities of a budget accountant will vary according to the organisation, typically the role involves preparing the budgets, monitoring the budgets against actual performance and reporting on the variances. The budget accountant's role should be outlined in the budget manual, and may have the following responsibilities:

- advise and assist functional managers in their budget submissions
- liaise with the budget committee and ensure that all budgeting activities are carried out in line with the budget manual
- ensure that all budgets are fully coordinated
- ensure that agreed budgets are communicated to functional managers and deal with any queries
- monitor budgets against actual performance and prepare reports on significant variances
- ensure that the budget timetable is followed by all participants

budget timetables

There are two main types of budgets used by organisations:

- **strategic** budgets
- **operational** budgets

They have different purposes, and are each based on different timescales. The budget committee will typically determine the way that these budgets are set and monitored, in line with the budget manual.

Strategic budgets will be produced well in advance of the period to which they relate. They are concerned with the long-term strategy of the organisation, and will therefore have the following features:

- they relate to long periods of time (typically five years)

- they are prepared a long time in advance of the budget periods

- they are limited to outline information and are not set out in great detail

- they are the responsibility of the senior management of the organisation

Some organisations may adopt a rolling programme of strategic budgets, perhaps five years ahead. Each year a further year would be incorporated into the far end of the budget.

Operational budgets will be produced for shorter periods of time – typically the next twelve months. They may be developed from the original strategic budgets for the budget period, but will take account of the fact that the business has information – facts and figures – about the immediate future. Operating budgets will therefore have the following features:

- they relate to short periods of time (typically the forthcoming year, divided into manageable control periods)

- they are agreed a relatively short time in advance of the budget period (typically several months before the year starts)

- they are set up and agreed in considerable detail

- they are the responsibility of the middle managers that control the operations of the organisation

capital expenditure budgets

The overall strategic and operational budgets must include **capital expenditure budgets** as well as revenue budgets. Capital expenditure can range from straightforward replacement of equipment, to moving to new premises or acquiring whole businesses. Capital expenditure can be defined as expenditure on assets that will benefit the organisation over more than one accounting period. In addition to following this general rule, many organisations will also set out a minimum cost of assets that are to be treated as capital. This is to avoid low value items that appear to satisfy the definition being treated as capital (for example a calculator or an electric kettle). The minimum cost of a capital item could be set at (say) £200, or for a larger organisation, perhaps £2,000. This amount would be set out in the organisation's policy documents. The co-ordination of the capital expenditure budget is particularly important to ensure that:

- replacement equipment is acquired at the most cost-effective point for the organisation (before the old equipment becomes too costly to maintain, but not until the replacement is justified)

- planned production output that relies on capital expenditure is properly incorporated into both the appropriate revenue budgets and into the capital expenditure budget

- other resources are available to coordinate with the capital expenditure (for example installation, raw materials to cope with increased output)

- the labour requirements are available, and the workforce suitably trained

- suitable funding has been obtained to meet the capital expenditure

- appropriate planning has been carried out to phase in the use of the new non-current (fixed) assets

effective budgeting

The budgeting system must involve honesty, openness and transparency if it is to be effective. The system must be fair to all participants, and also be seen to be fair. Where decisions have to be made by senior managers about projects to be funded and the level of support to be provided to departments, the decision making process must be clearly laid out and then followed by all concerned. The opportunity for managers to feel that they have been badly treated by the process must be minimised by ensuring that the entire system is transparent.

For example, suppose the distribution manager has requested capital expenditure to replace the delivery vehicles, and the production manager has requested that some outdated manufacturing equipment also be replaced. If resources are limited, the procedure for deciding which capital expenditure should have priority should be objective and transparent and based on the best result for the whole organisation. In that way there can be no accusations of favouritism.

Where systems are not open and transparent individual managers who feel that their projects or requests have not been treated fairly are likely to become disillusioned and demotivated. Similarly, if a manager is believed to have submitted over-optimistic forecasts in support of a project that he is advocating then this will result in grievances being felt by other managers. There may be a role for the budget accountant in ensuring that data submitted is accurate and can withstand independent scrutiny.

PRODUCING MASTER BUDGETS

It was explained in the previous chapter that communication and coordination are key purposes of budgeting. The creation of a set of master budgets brings together the data from all the subsidiary budgets into a budgeted statement of profit or loss together with budgeted statement of financial position and a cash budget. In this way all the budgets are coordinated and the results can be communicated to all parties. It enables all budgets to be checked for viability. For example, the sales budget must be achievable and link to production schedules that can be met and inventory levels that can be managed. The impact of all the budgets must be a budgeted level of financial performance (including profitability) that is appropriate. This must be achievable without putting undue pressure on the financial position (company assets and liabilities) or the organisation's liquidity (having sufficient cash and other resources to meet its financial obligations).

The following Case Study will reinforce the process, and demonstrate how the various budgets are coordinated. The term 'operating budget' can be used to describe a budgeted statement of profit or loss that ends with 'operating profit' (or loss).

Case Study

COORDINATION LIMITED: DEVELOPING AN OPERATING BUDGET

situation

Coordination Limited manufactures and sells a single product for £28.00 per unit. It has already developed a production budget (in units) for period 3, based on forecast sales of 13,000 units, together with anticipated finished goods inventory levels. The production budget for period 3 shows scheduled production of 12,800 units.

Materials:

Each unit takes 3.5 kilos of material to manufacture. The inventory of material at the start of period 3 is budgeted to be 22,400 kilos (valued at £39,200), and at the end of period 3 to be 25,600 kilos. The budgeted purchase price of material is £1.80 per kilo in period 3, and this cost is also to be used to value the closing inventory.

Labour:

Each unit takes 45 minutes to produce. 50 staff each work 180 basic hours in the period at a cost of £12.00 per labour hour. Overtime is available at a rate of £15.00 per labour hour.

Overhead:

Variable overhead is absorbed at a rate of £2.80 per labour hour worked. Fixed overhead is budgeted at £9,560 for the period.

Operating Budget:

The budgeted opening inventory of finished goods has already been calculated as 2,500 units valued at £17.60 per unit. The closing inventory is to be valued at production cost per unit.

Administration costs are budgeted at £26,500 for the period and Marketing costs at £15,700.

required

- Complete a materials budget showing both kilos and value of inventories, purchases and amounts used in production.
- Complete a labour budget, showing time and costs of basic hours and overtime.
- Complete an overhead budget showing variable, fixed and total overhead for the period.
- Complete an operating budget for the period.

solution

Materials Budget:

	Kilos	£
Opening inventory	22,400	39,200
Purchases	48,000	86,400
Sub-total	70,400	125,600
Used in production	44,800	79,520
Closing inventory	25,600	46,080

Workings:

The order of calculation is important in this situation:

- The opening inventory (kilos and value) is given and can be inserted.
- The kilos used in production is calculated as 12,800 units x 3.5 kg = 44,800.
- The sub-total will equal the quantity used in production, plus the closing inventory 44,800 + 25,600 = 70,400 kilos.
- This sub-total will also equal the opening inventory plus purchases, so the purchases must be 70,400 – 22,400 = 48,000 kilos.
- The purchases can now be valued at 48,000 x £1.80 = 86,400.
- The value sub-total can be calculated as £39,200 + £86,400 = £125,600
- The closing inventory is also valued at purchase price (from the Case Study instructions) 25,600 x £1.80 = £46,080.
- The value of material used in production must therefore be £125,600 – £46,080 = £79,520.

Labour Budget:

	Hours	£
Basic rate	9,000	108,000
Overtime	600	9,000
Total	9,600	117,000

Workings:

This is more straightforward than the materials budget.

- The total hours needed for production is calculated at 12,800 x 45/60 = 9,600 hours.
- The basic rate hours are 50 employees x 180 hours = 9,000 hours.
- The balance is made up of overtime hours 9,600 – 9,000 = 600 hours.
- The values are calculated for basic rate (9,000 x £12 = £108,000) and overtime (600 x £15 = £9,000).
- The total cost is £108,000 + £9,000 = £117,000.

Overhead Budget:

	£
Variable overhead: 9,600 hours x £2.80	26,880
Fixed overhead	9,560
Total overhead	36,440

Operating Budget

	£	£
Sales revenue		364,000
Cost of goods sold:		
Opening inventory of finished goods		44,000
Cost of production:		
Materials	79,520	
Labour	117,000	
Overhead	36,440	
		232,960
Closing inventory of finished goods		41,860
Cost of goods sold		235,100
Gross profit		128,900
Administration	26,500	
Marketing	15,700	
		42,200
Operating profit		86,700

Particular care needs to be taken with the valuation of closing inventory. Full workings for the operating budget are as follows:

- Sales revenue is 13,000 units x £28.00 = £364,000.

- Opening inventory of finished goods is 2,500 x £17.60 = £44,000.

- Materials, labour and overheads are taken from the budgets prepared earlier, and totalled to arrive at a cost of production of £232,960.

- The cost of production of £232,960 is divided by the 12,800 units made to give a production cost of £18.20 per unit to be used to value closing inventory.

- The closing inventory of finished goods in units is calculated as 13,000 – (2,500 + 12,800) = 2,300. This is valued at production cost of £18.20 to give a valuation of £41,860.

- The cost of goods sold is £44,000 + £232,960 – £41,860 = £235,100.

- The gross profit is £364,000 – £235,100 = £128,900.

- Administration and marketing amounts are inserted, totalled, and deducted from gross profit to arrive at the budgeted operating profit of £86,700.

Note that while all the budget formats used above are typical, there may be variations, and extra care must be taken if the format is unfamiliar.

CASH BUDGET

The cash budget is an important budget which illustrates the effect on cash flow of all the other budgets (including the capital expenditure budget). Cash budgets are usually prepared on a month by month basis so that fluctuations in cash balances can be anticipated and plans made for short-term borrowing or investment if necessary. A typical format is shown opposite, including sample figures. The actual descriptions of the receipts and payments will be tailored to the organisations' needs.

The key to preparing an accurate cash budget is to base it on the time that cash will be received or paid. This must take account of lagging – the difference in time between sales being invoiced and cash being received, and between purchases being made or expenses being incurred and when payments are made. You may be told, for example, that purchases are paid for after two months. It is also possible that receipts or payments may be split in terms of timing. For example, half of customers could take one month to pay and half take two months.

It is also vital to remember that 'non-cash' items are not recorded in a cash budget. Depreciation is the most important example of non-cash expenditure. However the initial purchase of non-current assets does need to be recorded in a cash budget, as do other non-operational payments like dividends and taxation.

Cash Budget	January £	February £	March £	April £
Receipts				
Receipts from Sales	10,000	12,000	10,500	15,000
Other Receipts		14,000		
Total Receipts	10,000	26,000	10,500	15,000
Payments				
Materials	5,000	4,800	5,200	4,300
Labour	4,100	3,800	4,000	4,250
Production Overheads	1,100	1,200	1,050	1,150
Administration Costs	500	450	480	500
Non-current Assets		12,500		
Dividends				7,000
Taxation	5,300			
Total Payments	16,000	22,750	10,730	17,200
Cash Flow for Month	(6,000)	3,250	(230)	(2,200)
Cash Balance b/f	10,000	4,000	7,250	7,020
Cash Balance c/f	4,000	7,250	7,020	4,820

worked example

The following budget has been prepared for Quarter 1 (January to March).

	January £	February £	March £
Sales	55,000	43,500	61,500
Materials	15,000	14,000	16,300
Labour	11,000	8,700	12,300
Overheads	10,000	10,000	10,000
Gross Profit	19,000	10,800	22,900

All sales are made on two months' credit.

Materials are purchased on one months' credit.

There is no inventory of materials.

Labour is paid for in the month that it is incurred.

Overheads include monthly depreciation of £4,000. Payments for overheads are made in the month incurred.

Required: Show the cash receipts and payments for March.

Solution:

		£
Receipts from Sales	(January Sales)	55,000
Payments for materials	(February purchases)	14,000
Payments for Labour	(March labour)	12,300
Payments for overheads	(£10,000 – £4,000)	6,000

One way that receipts and payments can be calculated is to make use of our knowledge of how opening and closing balances interact with sales, purchases and expenses.

For example, if we know the forecast opening and closing trade receivables for a period as well as the expected sales, we can calculate what the receipts from sales should be. The receipts should equal (opening trade receivables + sales – closing trade receivables). You have probably used this idea in your other studies.

We can use similar calculations to work out payments for materials involving inventory movements (materials used – opening inventory, + closing inventory). If there are trade payables (or accruals) involved the calculation will be (purchases + opening trade payables – closing trade payables).

Case Study

CASHET LIMITED:
CASH BUDGET

The company has prepared the following operating budget for the next period:

	£	£
Sales Revenue		306,000
Less Expenditure:		
Materials	110,000	
Labour	123,500	
Depreciation	25,000	
Expenses	34,000	
		292,500
Operating Profit		13,500

The following amounts are forecast in the statements of financial position at the start and end of the period:

	Start £	End £
Trade Receivables	45,400	50,100
Materials Inventory	21,450	22,500
Labour Accruals	2,000	1,500
Expense Prepayments	12,400	13,100
Bank	43,500	

required

Complete the summary cash flow budget for the period.

solution

	Cash Flow Budget £	Workings for information £
Receipts from sales	301,300	306,000 + 45,400 − 50,100
Payments for materials	111,050	110,000 − 21,450 + 22,500
Payments for labour	124,000	123,500 + 2,000 − 1,500
Payments for expenses	34,700	34,000 − 12,400 + 13,100
Total payments	269,750	
Net cash flow	31,550	
Balance b/f	43,500	
Balance c/f	75,050	

PERFORMANCE MEASUREMENT

When budgets are being created and agreed it is important to ensure that they are in line with acceptable performance measures. It would not make sense to plan for outcomes that do not provide the financial returns that the organisation needs.

As well as making sure that the budgets reflect required levels of operating profit and return on capital employed, each element of income and cost must be agreed as appropriate. Once the budget is in place and actual performance is being monitored, the same performance indicators can be used to compare the actual performance with that in the budget.

Budgeted sales will reflect the following elements:

■ unit sales, possibly split across markets or geographical areas

■ average selling price per unit

■ percentage discount offered (if any)

■ percentage market share

Using materials as a cost example, the types of performance measurement that must be built into the original budgets include:

■ price per kilo of materials

■ material usage per unit of production

■ percentage wastage

■ materials inventory

Similarly, direct labour would include the following performance measures that can also be used later to monitor actual outcomes:

■ average hourly rate paid

■ average labour time taken to produce each unit of output

■ percentage unproductive time

The above are only examples – you can probably think of other useful performance measures. We will consider performance measurement again later in this book when we examine monitoring actual performance.

BUDGET SUBMISSION

When budgets are being prepared it is important that all parties involved are aware of the assumptions that have been made. Clear communication is vital, and you may be required to select the appropriate information to use to notify managers about the budget.

You may need to check your understanding of data that has been provided before using it, and then to set out the results of your work in a clear, understandable and professional manner. Budgets are important documents, and all those who are providing an input must appreciate the implications of what is being put forward.

For example, the person preparing the budget for materials would normally liaise with both the purchasing manager and the production manager to ensure that both the prices and usages being used were accurate. If one of these managers was not available it would not be appropriate to simply make a guess at key figures and hope that it would all be alright!

The budget holder is the manager who will be accountable for the budget and for the subsequent actual performance which will be monitored against the budget. It is vital that the budget being submitted to the budget committee is endorsed by the budget holder, who does so based on full understanding of the implications of the budget. It will probably be one of the roles of the budget accountant to ensure that the budget holders are fully aware of their budget responsibilities and to deal with any queries that they may raise.

The next Case Study illustrates the kind of communication that may be appropriate when explaining assumptions and seeking approval for a budget or part of a budget.

Case Study

AGREE LIMITED: COMMUNICATING BUDGET ASSUMPTIONS

You have prepared a draft budget for direct labour costs.

- It is based on this year's costs plus an expected pay rise and increased staffing.
- The manager of human resources has forecast the pay rise.
- You have calculated the required staffing from the agreed production budget.

Direct labour budget

	This year	Next year
Production units	780,000	820,000
Minutes per unit	6.00	6.00
Labour hours	78,000	82,000
Annual hours per staff member	1,800	1,800
Number of staff	44	46
Average salary p.a.	£25,000	£26,500
Direct labour cost	£1,100,000	£1,219,000

required

Write an email to the Production Director, explaining the calculations and assumptions and requesting his approval.

solution

> To: Production Director
>
> From: Accounting Technician
>
> Date: 23/10/20-5
>
> Direct Labour Budget
>
> **Budget submission**
>
> I attach the proposed direct labour budget for next year for your consideration and approval.
>
> The agreed production plan indicates an increase in volume from 780,000 to 820,000 units next year. No change in productivity has been assumed. Therefore, the staffing level needs to increase from 44 to 46.
>
> The manager of human resources estimates that average pay will increase by 6% next year from £25,000 to £26,500.
>
> Please let me know if you need any further information.

Chapter Summary

- The way in which budgets are used in an organisation is often laid down in the budget manual. In many organisations the responsibility for budget setting and control will rest with the Budget Committee. This will incorporate senior representatives of all major parts of the organisation to ensure full co-ordination.

- Budgets for manufacturing organisations can be created by working from the forecast sales data to the production level by using anticipated finished goods inventory levels. From the production budget the materials usage can be ascertained, and by incorporating the anticipated materials inventory levels the materials purchases can be calculated. Master budgets, the budgeted operating statement and cash budget, can also be created from the production budget.

- Budgets must be created to match expected performance measures, so that these can also be used later on to monitor actual performance.

- Budget holders must understand the budgets that they are submitting for approval and appreciate that they will be accountable for both the budgets and the actual performance.

Key Terms		
	budget committee	a committee charged with the responsibility of setting and monitoring the budget. It will include senior representatives from all parts of the organisation
	budget manual	a document containing information about how an organisation's policy on budgeting is implemented
	strategic budget	a long-term budget produced in outline only
	operational budget	a short-term budget produced in detail
	capital expenditure budget	budget detailing approved expenditure on assets that will benefit the organisation for more than one accounting period
	budgeted operating statement	budget based on the statement of profit or loss, showing the detail making up budgeted operating profit
	cash budget	budget showing planned cash flows over the budget period
	performance indicators	measurable items (including ratios) that show the performance that is planned in the budget
	budget holder	the manager responsible for a specific budget and the actual performance that is measured against that budget

Activities

4.1   Who would you contact in each of the following situations?

(a)   You want to identify the production capacity of the firm.

(b)   You want to forecast the price of raw materials.

(c)   The draft budget is ready for review.

Choose from:

- Trade union representative
- Managing director
- Buyer or purchasing manager
- Budget committee
- Production planning manager
- Marketing manager

4.2   An organisation has the following budgets:

- Personnel
- Cost of Production
- Maintenance
- Capital Expenditure
- Marketing

Select the most appropriate budget for each of the following costs:

(a)   Production wages

(b)   Printing recruitment application forms

(c)   Advertising

(d)   Customer demand survey

(e)   Raw materials

(f)   Spare parts for production machines

(g)   Warehouse extension

(h)   Sales commission paid to staff

4.3 You are required to complete the workings schedules and Operating Budget below.

The Operating Budget is another name for the Budget Income Statement.

Workings schedules

Materials	kg	£
Opening inventory	2,100	2,000
Purchases	15,500	27,125
Sub-total	17,600	29,125
Used		
Closing inventory	1,000	

Closing inventory of materials is to be valued at budgeted purchase price

Labour	Hours	£
Basic time @ £12 per hour		

It takes 4 minutes to make each item

Production Overhead	Hours	£
Variable @ £2.00 per labour hour		
Fixed		4,625
Total Production Overheads		

Operating budget

	units	£
Sales revenue @ £2.60 each	29,000	
Opening inventory of finished goods	4,000	7,000
Cost of production	30,000	
Materials		
Labour		
Production Overhead		
Total		
Closing inventory of finished goods*	5,000	

*Valued at budgeted production cost per unit

Cost of goods sold		
Gross profit		

Non-Production Overheads

Administration		3,000
Marketing		4,000
Total		7,000
Operating profit		

4.4 Consolidation Limited manufactures and sells a single product for £15.00 per unit. It has already developed a production budget (in units) for period 6, based on forecast sales of 7,000 units, together with anticipated finished goods inventory levels. The production budget for period 6 shows scheduled production of 6,850 units.

Materials:

Each unit takes 1.5 kilos of material to manufacture. The inventory of material at the start of period 6 is budgeted to be 2,055 kilos (valued at £2,135), and at the end of period 6 to be 2,100 kilos. The budgeted purchase price of material is £1.05 per kilo in period 6, and this cost is also to be used to value the closing inventory.

Labour:

Each unit takes 15 minutes to produce. 10 staff each work 165 basic hours in the period at a cost of £12.00 per labour hour. Overtime is available at a rate of £16.00 per labour hour. Total hours required must be rounded up to the next whole hour.

Overhead:

Variable overhead is absorbed at a rate of £3.00 per labour hour. Fixed overhead is budgeted at £8,497 for the period.

Operating Budget:

The budgeted opening inventory of finished goods has already been calculated as 2,000 units valued at £6.50 per unit. The closing inventory is to be valued at budgeted production cost per unit.

Administration costs are budgeted at £16,500 for the period and Marketing costs at £23,450.

Required:

- Complete a materials budget showing both kilos and value of inventories, purchases and amounts used in production.

- Complete a labour budget, showing time and costs of basic hours and overtime.

- Complete an overhead budget showing variable, fixed and total overhead for the period.

- Complete an operating budget for the period.

4.5 Prepare a Cash Budget for May from the following budget data

Budget data	March £	April £	May £	June £	Cash Budget	May £
Invoiced sales	6,000	7,000	6,600	7,600	Opening cash balance	(480)
					Receipts:	
Purchases	2,000	2,200	2,400	2,200	Customer receipts	
Wages	1,000	1,020	1,040	960		
Other cash overheads	1,200	1,320	1,240	1,260	**Payments:**	
Capital expenditure	0	2,400	0	0	For purchases	
					For wages	
Average terms					For overheads	
Half of customers take 1 month to pay. Half take 2 months.					For capital exp.	
Purchases paid for after two months					Total payments	
Wages paid in the current month						
Other cash overheads paid after one month					Closing cash balance	
Capital expenditure paid in the current month						

4.6 Produce a cash budget for the month of March from the following information:

Operating Budget for Month of March	£	£
Revenue		56,500
Costs:		
Materials	15,500	
Labour	19,500	
Expenses	14,650	
		49,650
Operating Profit		6,850

Assumptions for March:

Trade receivables will decrease by £2,000

Inventory of materials will increase by £1,200

Materials are payable in month of purchase

Wages are paid in current month

Expenses payable will decrease by £650

4.7 You have prepared the following draft direct labour budget for the coming year.

	Current Year (Actual)		Next Year (Budget)	
Production Units		19,500		20,100
	Hours	£	Hours	£
Basic Rate	25,500	331,500	28,900	390,150
Overtime Rate	3,750	73,125	1,853	37,523
Total	29,250	404,625	30,753	427,673

Further information:

The Personnel Manager has predicted an increase in the hourly rates.

There is an increase planned in the number of permanent staff, each one continues working 1,700 hours per year.

The Production Manager has allowed for an increase in the average time taken to produce each unit to allow for training of the new staff.

Required:

Write an email to the budget committee:

- Requesting approval of the budget and explaining the assumptions and their implications.

- Suggesting two appropriate performance indicators (together with their budgeted values) that can be used to monitor performance.

4.8 You have prepared a draft budget for direct labour costs.

- It is based on this year's costs plus an expected pay rise and increased staffing.

- The manager of human resources has forecast the pay rise.

- You have calculated the required staffing from the agreed production budget.

Direct labour budget	This year	Next year
Production units	780,000	820,000
Minutes per unit	6.00	6.00
Labour hours	78,000	82,000
Annual hours per staff member	1,800	1,800
Number of staff	44	46
Average salary p.a.	£25,000	£26,500
Direct labour cost	£1,100,000	£1,219,000

Required:

Write an email to the Production Director suggesting appropriate performance indicators for this budget.

5 Revising budgets

this chapter covers...

In this chapter we examine the various reasons why budgets may need to be revised, and how this can be carried out.

We start with dividing budgets into shorter periods. Here we have to be careful to use our knowledge of cost behaviour accurately, particularly when production output differs from the sales level.

The next section deals with how to revise a budget. This can be needed if alternative strategies are being considered, or if plans have changed since the original budget was created. The application of cost behaviour is also important for this process.

We then go on to discuss how constraints may impose changes on budgets, and what strategies can be used to minimise problems. We also see how product choice can be managed when there are limited resources.

Finally we examine how to deal with the uncertainty that is inherent in budgeting. This includes the use of sensitivity analysis, flexible budgets and rolling budgets.

DIVIDING BUDGETS INTO SHORTER PERIODS

You may be required to break down a budget that has been prepared for one long period into shorter periods. For example, you could be asked to arrive at a budget for a particular month by using an annual budget, together with other information.

To do this you must use the information provided carefully, and ensure that each calculation is based on a logical approach. It will not usually be appropriate to simply divide an annual budget by 12 to arrive at a monthly budget.

If you are presented with a budget that incorporates sales revenue and production costs you must ensure that:

- the sales revenue is broken down according to the sales information, and

- the costs of production are calculated according to the production levels (not the sales levels)

The following approach (which is based on your understanding of cost behaviour) should be used if you are presented with annual budgets and asked to show the budgets for a particular month (or week) within the year.

- the sales revenue budget is calculated based on the unit sales for the period, multiplied by the unit selling price. You may need to calculate the unit selling price from the annual figures by dividing the revenue by the number of units.

If you are asked to calculate costs that relate to the production (not the cost of sales) you need to be careful that you use the production output as your starting point, as follows:

- the materials budget is calculated using the production output multiplied by the material cost of each unit. This is based on the quantity of material needed to make one unit multiplied by the price (for example per kilo).

- the direct labour costs are based on the number of hours needed to make the expected production output. If there are different rates of pay (for example basic rate and overtime) you will need to establish how many hours are needed at each rate. This is the same process that we used when calculating labour budgets previously.

- variable overhead typically uses an hourly rate multiplied by the number of direct labour hours worked in the period (as just calculated for direct labour). You may need to calculate the hourly rate by using the annual variable overheads divided by the annual hours worked. Note that if (for example) time and a half is paid for overtime, the hours worked will not be the same as hours paid, so be careful to use the right number.

■ fixed overheads are usually considered as time-based costs, so the annual budget is often simply divided up on a time basis. This usually means simply dividing the annual costs by 12 to obtain a month (or 52 for a week), but watch out in case you are asked to take account of the number of days in a period.

The following Case Study will illustrate the approach.

Case Study

SPLITTER LIMITED: CALCULATING MONTHLY BUDGET

The budget shown below has been produced for the year 20-5.

In addition the following information is also available:

· Each unit is manufactured from 4kg of material, costing £2.50 per kg.

· It takes 6 minutes labour time to make each unit.

· 1,480 hours of labour at basic rate is available in June – excess hours must be paid at the overtime rate.

· Basic rate for labour is £15 per hour; overtime rate is £20 per hour.

· Variable production overheads relate to total labour hours worked.

· Fixed production overheads are spread evenly over the months of the year.

	Year	June
Units sold	240,000	18,000
Units produced	200,000	17,500
	£	£
Sales revenue	4,800,000	
Costs of production:		
Material usage	2,000,000	
Direct labour	360,000	
Variable production overhead	720,000	
Fixed production overhead	480,000	

required

Complete the table to show the sales revenue and cost of production budget for June 20-5.

solution

	Year	June
Units sold	240,000	18,000
Units produced	200,000	17,500
	£	£
Sales revenue	4,800,000	360,000
Costs of production:		
Material usage	2,000,000	175,000
Direct labour	360,000	27,600
Variable production overhead	720,000	63,000
Fixed production overhead	480,000	40,000

Workings:

Sales revenue: (£4,800,000 / 240,000) x 18,000 = £360,000

Material usage: £2.50 x 4kg x 17,500 = £175,000

Direct labour: Hours required = 17,500 x (6 / 60) = 1,750
                  1,480 x £15 = £22,200
                  270 x £20 = £5,400
                  £22,200 + £5,400 = £27,600

Variable overhead: (£720,000 / 20,000* annual hours) x 1,750 = £63,000

*annual hours = 200,000 units / 10 units per hour

Fixed overhead: £480,000 / 12 = £40,000

You may be asked to carry out a similar task involving splitting a cash budget into a shorter period. Use the knowledge that you gained in the previous chapter to ensure that you adopt a logical approach.

REVISING A BUDGET

It may sometimes be necessary to revise a budget either because the original budget is no longer appropriate, or to demonstrate the impact of an alternative strategy that needs to be considered.

Some of the techniques that you may need to use are cost behaviour (as covered in Chapter 1), and the use of percentage calculations (as explained in Chapter 2).

Revisions to a budget can include:

- changes to selling prices
- changes to sales and production volumes
- changes to costs

These changes may occur in combination (for example an increased selling price combined with a reduced volume) so care is needed to carry out the calculations accurately.

The approach is fairly similar to that just used for dividing budgets into shorter periods – the build-up of current budgeted income and costs needs to be understood and applied to the new situation.

Often tasks will either be presented in marginal costing format or will assume that the sales volume is identical to the production volume. In either case, the complication of production output differing from sales will not apply. The following notes are prepared on that basis.

The following process should be followed when revising a budget.

sales revenue

The sales revenue is made up of sales units multiplied by selling price per unit. The unadjusted selling price may be given to you, or you may need to calculate it from the existing figures. You may then be provided with a percentage increase or decrease to apply to the original selling price. This price change would often be in combination with a sales volume change. Typically the higher the price is, the lower the volume falls. The revised sales revenue will be made up of the new volume multiplied by the new selling price per unit.

materials

Material costs are also made up of volume multiplied by material price. Be careful to ignore any selling price changes here – they are not relevant. A step-by-step method of calculation can be used as follows. An existing material cost per unit is first calculated, then revised, and then applied to the revised volume (since this is a variable cost).

Alternatively, an all-in-one calculation can be used. Both are illustrated in this example.

worked example

Material costs in the original budget are shown as £542,500, based on volume of 155,000 units. The revised budget is to be for an increase in volume of 10%, together with a price increase imposed by the material supplier of 2%.

Method 1 Step-by-step

The current material cost per unit is £542,500 / 155,000 = £3.50

The revised material cost per unit will therefore be £3.50 x 102% = £3.57

The revised volume will be 155,000 x 110% = 170,500

The revised material cost will therefore be £3.57 x 170,500 = £608,685

Method 2 All-in-one

Revised material cost budget

= current material cost budget £542,500 x 102% x 110%   = £608,685

As you can see, both methods will arrive at the same answer – provided you are careful with the calculations!

labour

Provided the labour costs behave as variable costs, the calculations can be carried out in exactly the same alternative ways as explained above for material costs.

worked example

For example, direct labour costs are shown in the original budget as £750,000, based on volume of 155,000 units. Revised volume is to be 10% greater, and labour rate is to allow for an increase of 2.5%.

Using the all-in-one method gives a revised labour budget of:

£750,000 x 110% x 102.5% = £845,625.

In this example the step-by-step approach would result in a direct labour cost per unit that is not an exact number (even after 7 decimal places). If you find yourself in this situation, it's best to use the all-in-one method above.

stepped costs

Some costs may behave as stepped costs. The key to carrying out revised budgets in these situations is to realise that each step is normally based on **up to** a particular volume of units. For example if the original volume was 155,000, and each step of a certain cost was based on up to 15,000 units, then there would be 11 steps involved. Ten steps would take us up to 150,000 units maximum, but the extra 5,000 units requires another whole step.

worked example

Suppose the original volume of 155,000 is to be revised by an extra 10% (as in previous examples). The original budgeted cost is a total of £99,000, and increases regularly at every 15,000 units.

The original budget is based on 11 steps, so each step must have been for £99,000 / 11 = £9,000. The new volume is 155,000 x 110% = 170,500. This requires 12 steps (which takes us to a maximum 180,000).

The revised budget will therefore be 12 x £9,000 = £108,000.

fixed costs

Where costs are described as behaving as fixed costs, they will not alter for volume reasons provided the fixed volume range is not exceeded. If there is no mention of the range within which the costs are fixed, then you can assume that the costs are not influenced by volume. If a volume range is noted, be careful to apply any changes to the revised budget.

worked example

For example, suppose the fixed costs of £200,000 apply to volumes up to 160,000 units. If the volume exceeds 160,000 the fixed costs will increase by £5,000.

If the original volume of 155,000 units is increased by 10% to 170,500, the new fixed cost will be £200,000 + £5,000 = £205,000.

This is really another form of stepped cost – but with just one step, and of a given amount.

The following case study will illustrate the type of situation that you may be presented with.

Case Study

RE-VISION LIMITED: PREPARING A REVISED BUDGET

A draft operating budget has been submitted to the budget committee. The committee has requested that a revised budget is prepared based on an alternative scenario.

The assumptions made in developing the original budget were as follows:

- material and labour costs are variable
- an allowance has been made for a 2% increase in labour rates from the previous year
- production overheads is a stepped fixed cost, increasing regularly at every 20,000 units

The alternative scenario is based on the following assumptions:

- selling price will be reduced by 4%
- sales and production volume will increase by 10%
- material prices will increase by 3%
- labour rates will increase by 1% compared to the previous year

required

Complete the table on the next page to show the data and operating budget based on the alternative scenario.

Round figures (except selling price) to the nearest whole number if necessary.

Operating Budget	First Draft	Alternative Scenario
Selling price per unit	£8.00	
Sales and production volume	110,000	
	£	£
Sales revenue	880,000	
Production costs:		
Materials	220,000	
Labour	336,600	
Production overheads	120,000	
Total production costs	676,600	
Gross profit	203,400	

solution

Operating Budget	First Draft	Alternative Scenario
Selling price per unit	£8.00	£7.68
Sales and production volume	110,000	121,000
	£	£
Sales revenue	880,000	929,280
Production costs:		
Materials	220,000	249,260
Labour	336,600	366,630
Production overheads	120,000	140,000
Total production costs	676,600	755,890
Gross profit	203,400	173,390

Workings:

Selling price per unit:	£8.00 x 96%	= £7.68
Sales and production volume:	110,000 x 110%	=121,000
Sales revenue:	121,000 x £7.68	= £929,280
Material costs:		
(affected by volume and price)		
(£220,000 / 110,000) x 121,000 x 103%		= £249,260

Labour costs:
(affected by volume and rate)
(£336,600 / 110,000) x 121,000 x (100 / 102) x 101%   = £366,630

Production overheads:
Original cost is based on up to 120,000 units
Revised cost is based on up to 140,000 units
(£120,000 / 120,000) x 140,000   = £140,000

SALES AND PRODUCTION CONSTRAINTS

In this section we will discuss a variety of constraints that may prevent an organisation from selling and/or producing more goods. You should understand the range of possible limitations on output and be able to work out the impact.

limited market share

It is almost impossible for an organisation to be in a monopoly situation and have access to 100% of the possible market of a product or service. There will always be a limit on the percentage of the market that an individual organisation can sell to.

For example, a restaurant will always be competing with other local restaurants for a share of the market for people who wish to dine out. The market share that is achieved will depend on the success of the organisation's marketing as well as the number and quality of the competitors and their pricing structure. It must also be remembered that there will be a limit on the total market for diners in an area – this will depend on the population, its habits, and its disposable income.

Effective marketing will increase market share to a certain extent, but this will always come at a cost. Care must be taken to ensure that any marketing undertaken generates more benefits than costs.

limited finance

When organisations have limited access to finance it can have wide ranging effects on the sales and production levels.

■ sales on credit will be restricted if there is a lack of working capital to support a high level of receivables.

■ inventory levels may need to be restricted. This can increase the risk of shortages of finished goods needed for sales and a lack of raw materials may interrupt production. Bulk discounts may also be unobtainable if the organisation only has the finance to buy in small quantities.

■ capital expenditure may need to be reduced or stopped completely. This can lead to inefficient production and the inability to expand the business.

Access to finance will depend on the organisation's creditworthiness, and also on the economic outlook of the segment that it operates in as well as the country as a whole.

limited materials

Sometimes an organisation finds that it cannot obtain the amount of materials that it had planned to purchase. This could be due to a worldwide shortage, or to a more localised problem, perhaps just with the organisation's usual supplier. The problems with supplies could be simply temporary, or relate to a longer-term situation that is developing.

The range of tactics that can be used to overcome or lessen the effect of such problems includes the following, which can be used individually or in combination:

■ **Utilising raw material inventory.** The planned production can sometimes be maintained by simply running down raw material inventory. This will only work in the short term, and will depend on the current raw material inventory level.

■ **Utilising finished goods inventory.** If production needs to be reduced due to limited raw materials, sales may still be maintained if there are sufficient finished goods in inventory. This can also only be effective as a temporary measure.

■ **Finding an alternative supplier.** This may be an obvious solution, although there may be cost implications, as well as quality considerations.

■ **Substituting an alternative material.** Although some products can only be made from one material, for others there may be alternatives that could be used. Implications may include material cost and quality, as well as usage levels, including wastage. The labour force may also work less efficiently, and the suitability of current machinery and equipment would need to be considered.

■ **Reformulating the product.** Changing the formula for manufacture can be carried out so that less of the raw material that is in short supply will be used. Clearly the quality of the finished item would have to be carefully considered, and the customers would need to accept the revised specification. This may involve using more of other raw materials to compensate.

■ **Buying in finished goods.** This may be a possibility, although it begs the question of where the supplier of those goods obtained their raw materials. This solution would imply reducing in-house production, and losing profit. The organisation's manufacturing facilities would be under utilised, and the labour force may need to be laid off unless an alternative product could be made on the premises.

■ **Manufacturing an alternative product using different materials.** This may involve major changes in the whole production process. If it is to be a substitute for the previous product the new product must be designed and marketed to meet the same need, and customers will have to be persuaded of its merits.

limited labour

Where labour is in limited supply a range of alternative solutions are possible. Appropriate labour can usually be obtained eventually, even if it means paying a high rate and/or investing substantial amounts in training. Because of this, labour shortage problems are typically short-term ones. The range of ways to deal with a labour shortage includes:

■ **Overtime working.** Although this probably involves paying a premium rate it is a logical way to tackle a temporary problem.

■ **Utilising finished goods inventory.** If production needs to be reduced due to limited availability of labour, sales may still be maintained if there are sufficient finished goods in inventory. In the same way as dealing with an inventory shortage, this can also only be effective as a temporary measure.

■ **Using sub-contractors.** This could include self-employed or agency staff within the factory, or possibly sub-contracting parts of the production process to another organisation and location. The latter may be a major decision with other implications. Any use of sub-contractors will have cost implications, although the responsibility for work quality may also lie with the sub-contractor, which may offset some of the disadvantages.

■ **Buying-in finished goods.** This would be a major decision, and would have to be carefully costed. The loss of control over the production process would have to be considered, including quality issues and reliability of supply. It may also leave the organisation's own premises under-utilised.

■ **Improving labour efficiency.** Although probably only a very limited change could be made in the short term, in the longer term training or better equipment may improve efficiency. Internal or external experts may be able to direct the organisation as to the best way to maximise the output of its labour force.

limited production capacity

When demand for an organisation's products is likely to outstrip its capacity to supply then the likely solutions will depend on whether the problem is believed to be permanent or temporary.

permanent inability to supply

Permanent inability to supply sufficient goods to customers can be solved by the organisation:

- increasing capacity by expanding premises or relocating
- increasing selling prices to reduce demand (and increase profit)
- sub-contracting or buying-in finished goods

temporary inability to supply

There may be temporary capacity problems caused either by:

- unexpected demand, or
- regular seasonal variations in demand

These factors can be dealt with by application of the following techniques:

- **Manipulating finished goods inventory levels.** The most logical technique is to utilise spare capacity when it exists to build up inventory to deal with higher demand. This inventory can be used as a contingency against unexpected demand, or in anticipation of seasonal peaks. The cost of holding excess inventory should not be overlooked.

- **Shift working.** This will have the effect of spreading the fixed overheads over a greater production level, and therefore reducing the indirect cost per unit. The direct labour cost may increase through shift premium payments, and the net effect on costs would have to be calculated carefully.

- **Renting temporary premises or additional equipment.** There may be additional costs in these approaches that would need to be considered.

- **Sub-contracting, or buying in finished goods, or improving efficiency.** The implications are as discussed previously when examining materials and labour shortages.

combination of limitations

There may be occasions when there is a limit on not just one resource, but a combination of two or more.

For example, if we originally planned to make 5,000 units, but find that we only have sufficient labour for 4,800 units, and enough materials for 4,000 units, then materials is the most pressing problem. It would not make sense to bring in temporary staff while there was still a materials shortage. If we can solve the materials shortage problem, only then should we turn our attention to the labour limitation. The issue that most constrains the output (as materials does in this example) is sometimes known as the **binding constraint**.

PRODUCT CHOICE WHEN THERE ARE LIMITED RESOURCES

The final situation that we must be able to deal with when there are limited resources concerns selecting the most profitable products. The situation arises when it was originally planned to make a number of different products, but a shortage of some resource now makes the plan impossible. The resource that is preventing normal output is known as the **limiting factor**. The most common limiting factors are either materials or labour.

What we must do in these circumstances is to calculate which of our products gives us the most profitable use of the limited resources. The technique relies on marginal costing techniques, and even if the data is provided in a different form, you must first identify the variable costs for each product.

The full procedure to be adopted is as follows:

■ Using marginal costing, calculate the contribution per unit that each different product generates. This is carried out by subtracting the variable costs per unit from the selling price per unit. Fixed costs are ignored.

■ Identify the resource that is in short supply (the limiting factor), and how much of that resource is needed to make one unit of each different product. Divide the contribution per unit already calculated by the quantity of limited resource required to make a unit. This gives the contribution per unit of limiting factor.

■ Rank the possible products according to the value of the contribution per unit of limiting factor. Starting with the product ranked highest, schedule the production so that the expected demand is met for this product. Then schedule the next highest-ranking product, and so on until the limited resources are used up.

This technique will ensure that the quantities of different products manufactured will make the most profit from the limited resources. This does mean that some products will be made in reduced quantities, or not made at all. This will leave the demand from some customers unsatisfied, and the technique does not address any further implications of this policy. For example a customer of a product that may have production suspended could also be a valuable customer of other products. Suspension of manufacture could result in the customer cancelling their orders and finding an alternative supplier for all their requirements.

The Case Study that follows shows how the technique is used to schedule production so that the profit from using limited resources is maximised.

THE THREE COUNTIES COMPANY: CONTRIBUTION PER UNIT OF LIMITING FACTOR

The Three Counties Company manufactures three products, each using the same material. The budget data for quarter 2 (the next quarter) is as follows. (There is no budgeted finished goods inventory at the beginning or end of any quarter.)

Product	Demand	Costs per unit		
	(units)	Materials	Labour	Overheads
Gloucester	10,000	£25.00	£30.00	£60.00
Worcester	15,000	£50.00	£30.00	£60.00
Hereford	12,000	£15.00	£20.00	£40.00

The material costs £5.00 per kilo. Due to its short shelf life it must be used in the period that it is bought. The labour force is employed on a fixed contract that entitles them to a weekly pay of £350 for a guaranteed 40-hour week. The contract prohibits any overtime working. The overheads are a fixed cost.

The Gloucester sells for £125 per unit, the Worcester for £150 per unit, and the Hereford for £90 per unit.

It has just been discovered that there is a limit on the quantity of material that can be purchased in quarter 2 of 180,000 kilos.

required
Produce a revised production budget in units for quarter 2 that maximises profit.

solution
Since the labour force is paid a guaranteed week the cost of labour behaves as a fixed cost in this Case Study. Because overheads are also fixed, the only variable cost is material. This gives contributions per unit calculations as follows:

	Gloucester £	Worcester £	Hereford £
Selling Price per unit	125	150	90
less variable costs	25	50	15
contribution per unit	100	100	75

The quantity of material used for each product can be calculated by dividing the cost of material for a unit by the cost per kilo of £5.00. This quantity is then used to calculate the contribution per kilo of material (the limiting factor).

	Gloucester	**Worcester**	**Hereford**
Quantity of material per unit	5 kg	10 kg	3 kg
Contribution per kilo of material	£100 / 5	£100 / 10	£75 / 3
	= £20	= £10	= £25
Ranking	2	3	1

The ranking is derived directly from the contribution per kilo of material. Note that this ranking is different from both the contribution per unit and from the profit per unit if calculated under absorption costing. We now use the ranking to produce up to the demand level of first the Hereford, followed by the Gloucester, and finally the Worcester, using up the material until there is none left.

Product	Ranking	Production (units)	Material Required (kilos)		
Hereford	1	12,000	12,000 x 3 kg	=	36,000
Gloucester	2	10,000	10,000 x 5 kg	=	50,000
Worcester	3	9,400*	9,400 x 10 kg	=	94,000
					180,000

*The quantity of Worcester that can be produced is calculated as follows:
First, the remaining quantity of material is calculated in kilos:
(180,000 − 36,000 − 50,000 = 94,000)
Then the number of Worcester that can be produced with that material is calculated:
(94,000 kg / 10 kg each unit = 9,400 units).

DEALING WITH UNCERTAINTY

Because data produced from forecasts is inherently uncertain, organisations must use techniques to minimise the risks of basing budgets on inaccurate forecasts. There are several methods available, and managers may use one or more of them.

One method is to use 'sensitivity analysis' to model the impact of using different forecasts. This is closely allied to the 'scenario planning' or 'what-if analysis' technique that you may have studied. For example, if the employees' pay level is not yet determined for the budget period, then alternative budgets based on (say) current pay levels, increases of 2%, or increases of 4% could be drafted to evaluate the impact.

Another method could be to update forecasts regularly to ensure that recent events are taken into account. As the initial forecasts may be completed well in advance of the budget period, it would make sense to see if they are still valid as the budget period approaches. For example, a sales forecast based on trend analysis may initially be developed using historical data that ceases a year before the budget period. By re-forecasting using more recent sales data as it becomes available, the managers can reassure themselves that the forecast being used is still valid, or if not they can make appropriate changes to their plans.

Many organisations prepare one set of budgets for planning purposes, known as **fixed budgets**. An alternative is to prepare a range of budgets, each based on a different level of activity (typically sales). These are known as **flexible budgets**, and demonstrate the impact of different sales volumes on the budgets. Having prepared the range of budgets, an organisation may commit to one of the budgets as being its financial plan (and have all the managers working towards it), while still being aware of the impacts of achieving different sales levels.

Even when fixed budgets are used for planning purposes, flexible budgets are often used for monitoring and control purposes. This is so there is a fair comparison between the costs actually incurred and the budgeted costs for the same activity (or sales) level. We will examine this use of flexible budgets in Chapter 6.

rolling budgets

Rolling budgets are used by some organisations. They consist of budgets that are continually extended into the future as time moves on. For example, a twelve month budget could initially be prepared for 1 January to 31 December. As the organisation moves through January, the budget would be extended at the far end by a further month, so that a budget for 1 February to 31 January is created. This process would be continued each month (or other agreed period) so that there is always the same length of budget extending into the future.

This can provide improved accuracy and responsiveness compared to traditional static budgets, as information on actual performance can be fed into the budgets much more quickly. If necessary the budget for the existing period (for example February to December using our earlier dates) can also be updated when the budget is extended. Rolling budgets are particularly useful for organisations that operate in fast-changing environments.

The disadvantages are that budgeting becomes time-consuming (and therefore expensive) and there may be confusion over trying to achieve ever moving targets if the existing budgets are constantly updated. This can lead to demotivation and the danger of participants putting the minimum effort into the budgeting process.

Chapter Summary

- After the initial budget submission, budgets often have to be revised for a variety of reasons. Annual budgets may need to be divided into shorter periods, or revised altogether to take account of changing circumstances or alternative strategies.

- Situations may develop where an organisation cannot obtain sufficient resources to carry out its intentions. Such constraints can range from limited market share, access to finance or shortages of materials, labour or production capacity. There are a variety of strategies that can be used to deal with these situations.

- Sensitivity analysis, flexible budgeting and rolling budgets are some of the methods that can be used to help deal with uncertainty in the budgeting process.

Key Terms

limiting factor	the factor that prevents the original planned production from being carried out. Examples of limiting factors are the available resources of direct materials or direct labour
contribution per unit of output	the variable costs per unit subtracted from the selling price per unit. This would be calculated separately for each different product. It is a concept used in marginal costing
contribution per unit of limiting factor	the contribution per unit of output divided by the quantity of the limiting factor that is required to manufacture one unit of the output. This would be calculated separately for each different product. Examples are contribution per kilo (or litre) of direct material and contribution per direct labour hour
sensitivity analysis	the use of modelling to assess the impact on budgets of various different volumes, prices and costs
fixed budgets	a set of budgets based on a single set of assumptions about sales levels; these budgets are often used for planning purposes
flexible budgets	a series of sets of budgets based on different sales levels; these may be used for anticipating different outcomes at the planning stage, or for monitoring actual costs against an appropriate budget
rolling budget	Budgets that are continually extended into the future as time goes on

Activities

5.1   Calculate the Sales Budget and the budgets that make up Cost of Production for April.

	Budget for the year	Budget for April
Units sold	24,000	2,000
Units produced	25,000	2,500
	£	£
Sales	480,000	
Costs of Production:		
Materials used	160,000	
Labour	120,000	
Variable production overhead	30,000	
Fixed overhead	1,800	
Total cost of Production	311,800	

Each unit is made from 4 kg of material costing £1.60 per kg.

It takes 24 minutes to make each item.

Labour costs £12 per hour.

Fixed overhead costs are incurred evenly through the year.

5.2 Calculate the Sales Budget, and the budgets that make up the Cost of Production for week 9.

	Budget for the year	Budget for week 9
Units sold	350,000	7,100
Units produced	360,000	7,000
	£	£
Sales	7,000,000	
Costs of Production:		
Materials used	1,944,000	
Labour	1,214,200	
Variable production overhead	1,260,000	
Fixed production overhead	780,000	
Total cost of production	5,198,200	

Each unit is made from 3 litres of material costing £1.80 per litre.

It takes 15 minutes to make each unit. There are 1,600 labour hours available each week at a basic rate of £13.00 per hour. Any hours required over this are paid at an overtime rate of 1.5 times basic rate.

Fixed production overhead accrues evenly over the year.

5.3 Supervision is a stepped fixed cost for a particular organisation. Each supervisor can manage the production of up to 20,000 units in a year. The cost of supervision is budgeted at £360,000 when annual output is 170,000 units.

Calculate the budgeted cost of supervision for annual unit production of:

(a) 160,000 units

(b) 175,000 units

(c) 185,000 units

5.4 A company has already produced budgets based on its first scenario.

Assumptions in the first scenario:

Materials and labour are variable costs

Depreciation is a stepped fixed cost increasing every 12,000 units

Occupancy costs and energy costs behave as fixed costs

There is an allowance for an energy price rise of 3%

The alternative scenario is based on:

An increase in selling price of 2%

A decrease in sales volume of 4%

An energy price decrease of 1%

An increase in occupancy costs of 4%

Apart from the selling price per unit, do not enter any decimals. Round to the nearest whole number if necessary.

Complete the alternative scenario column in the operating budget table and calculate the increase or decrease in expected profit.

Operating Budget	First Scenario	Alternative Scenario
Selling price per unit	£17.00	
Sales volume	150,000	
	£	£
Sales revenue	2,550,000	
Costs:		
Materials	600,000	
Labour	637,500	
Depreciation	312,000	
Energy	123,600	
Occupancy costs	235,000	
Total costs	1,908,100	
Operating profit	641,900	
Increase / (decrease) in profit		

5.5 A manufacturer has a temporary shortage of direct labour. Consideration is being given to either using overtime working of the remaining staff, or sub-contracting part of the manufacturing process to another organisation.

Suggest possible advantages and disadvantages of each approach.

5.6 A company has budgeted to make and sell 200,000 units in the coming year.

Each unit takes 0.5 labour hours to make and requires 2kg of raw material.

The quality control department can test 16,000 units each month.

A contract has been placed to purchase 300,000kg of raw material at an agreed price.

Further supplies can be obtained on the open market but the price is likely to be much higher.

The company employs 50 production workers. Each worker works 1,750 hours a year in normal time.

Complete the following analysis.

There is labour available to make . . . . units in normal time. Therefore, ... hours of

overtime will be needed.

The raw material contract will provide enough material to make . . . . units. Therefore, . . .

. . . . kg will have to be purchased on the open market.

Quality control can test . . . . units in the year. It will be necessary to make alternative

arrangements for . . . . units.

5.7 The Two Cities Company manufactures two products, each using the same material and the same direct labour force.

The original budget data for month 6 is as follows. There is no budgeted finished goods inventory at the beginning or end of any month.

Product	Demand	Costs per unit		
	(units)	Materials	Labour	Overheads
Bristol	2,000	£70.00	£18.00	£80.00
Cardiff	2,500	£60.00	£12.00	£40.00

The material costs £10.00 per kilo. The labour force is paid on an hourly basis at £6 per hour, and can be called in to work as appropriate. They have no minimum agreed working week, and will be sent home if there is no work available. Because of the nature of the contract there is no overtime premium payable. The overheads are a fixed cost.

The Bristol sells for £178 per unit, and the Cardiff for £150 per unit.

Following negotiations with the company management regarding conditions of employment, a number of the direct labour workers have decided to withdraw their labour. This leaves a reduced number of employees willing to work normally. It is estimated that the maximum number of working hours available from those working normally is 7,100 hours in month 6.

Required:

Produce a revised production budget in units for month 6 that maximises profit.

6 Monitoring and controlling performance with budgets

this chapter covers...

In this chapter we examine how budgets can be used for comparison with actual performance and appropriate action taken.

We start by looking in detail at how flexed budgets can be developed, which will then provide a fair version of the budget against which to compare actual income and costs. We also remind ourselves how the marginal costing format can be used in this context.

The next section discusses reasons for variances, and links back to the ideas of controllable costs that were discussed earlier. We then go on to see how standard costing can be used in conjunction with budgeting, and how flexed budget variances can be divided up into those relating to price and those relating to quantity of input.

The final sections in this chapter relate to management issues. The involvement in budget setting is discussed along with the implications of using budgets to motivate managers. We also see how the budgeting cycle can be used to develop a system of continuous improvement provided prompt and appropriate management action is taken.

FLEXIBLE BUDGETS AND VARIANCES

In order to monitor and control performance we need to compare actual results with budgeted results. Before we carry out the comparison we first need to ensure that the budget assumes the same level of activity as what actually occurred. In many situations the original 'fixed' budget will be for a different activity level, and so we will need to produce a 'flexible' budget.

A budget adjusted for a change in level of activity is called a 'flexed' or 'flexible' budget, which is more suitable if actual results are to be compared with budgets for the purposes of performance measurement, because it would mean that the comparison is of 'like with like'.

In order to prepare a flexible budget for revenue and costs, we need sufficient information to be able to calculate, for each element of cost:

■ the variable cost per unit of activity

■ the total fixed part of the cost

Some costs may be entirely variable or entirely fixed. For those which are semi-variable, the high-low method can be used if we have enough data. Some costs may behave as stepped fixed costs, and we must be able to adjust these costs. Once the costs have been analysed in this way, a budget can be prepared for any level of activity.

The cost behaviour identified may only apply within a relevant range, however, and therefore it may not be realistic to 'flex' the budget for very large changes in levels of activity.

A flexed budget is useful for preparing a performance report, where the actual costs and income are compared with the flexed budget applicable to the actual level of activity. Differences are shown in a 'variance' column, labelled as adverse or favourable. This form of report gives meaningful variances and is more acceptable to the person responsible for the budget.

preparing a flexible budget

To produce a flexible budget for the required level of activity, the total for each element of cost is calculated using:

■ total variable cost = variable cost per unit x number of units

■ total fixed cost remains unchanged

■ total semi-variable cost =

  Fixed part of cost + variable cost per unit x number of units

■ if, in a given case, there are any additional fixed costs which are incurred at certain levels of activity, or any step costs, these must be set at the correct level for the activity level of the flexed budget

MAC LIMITED:
BUDGETED COSTS

Mac Ltd manufactures a single product – a raincoat – using automated processes. The costs of production are budgeted, as shown in the table below, for outputs of 20,000 units per year and for 30,000 units per year.

Direct Labour consists of machine operatives' wages and the total wages behave as a step cost:

Output	Total Direct Labour
Up to 15,000 units	£20,000
Over 15,000 and up to 25,000 units	£35,000
Over 25,000 and up to 35,000 units	£50,000

Mac Limited: Budgeted Production Costs			
Output (units)	20,000	27,000	30,000
	£000s	£000s	£000s
Direct Material	140		210
Direct Labour	35		50
Machine running costs	90		110
Other production overheads	100		100
Total Production Cost	365		470

required

Complete the Budgeted Production Costs table by calculating the budgeted costs for Mac Ltd for output of 27,000 units. Note that Direct Labour is the only step cost.

solution

Mac Limited: Budgeted Production Costs			
Output (units)	20,000	27,000	30,000
	£000s	£000s	£000s
Direct Material W1	140	189	210
Direct Labour W2	35	50	50
Machine running costs W3	90	104	110
Other production overheads W4	100	100	100
Total Production Cost	365	443	470

workings

(see working note references in the table above)

W1 Direct Material is a variable cost:

£140,000 ÷ 20,000 = £210,000 ÷ 30,000 = £7

Therefore Direct Material = £7 per unit and £7 x 27,000 = £189,000.

W2 Direct Labour is a step cost, as given, and for 27,000 units it would be at the level of £50,000.

W3 Machine running costs are semi-variable, because they do not change in line with output. Using the high-low method:

	Cost	Units		
High	£110,000	30,000		
Low	£90,000	20,000		
Difference	£20,000	÷	10,000	= £2 per unit

Fixed cost = £90,000 – (£2 x 20,000) = £50,000

Total cost for 27,000 units = £50,000 + (£2 x 27,000) = £104,000.

W4 Other production overheads are fixed at £100,000.

In the previous Case Study we illustrated how costs can be adjusted to create a flexible budget. We will now examine how both income and costs can be adjusted, and how the flexible budget can then be compared with the actual costs to produce meaningful variances.

Case Study

FLEXIE LIMITED:
FLEXIBLE BUDGET AND VARIANCES

The original March budget for Flexie Limited assumed sales of 30,000 units. The actual sales were 32,500 units. The following information is available about the budgeted costs:

- Materials, labour and distribution costs are variable.
- Energy costs are semi-variable. The variable element is £3 per unit.
- Equipment hire is a stepped cost. Each step is based on up to 3,000 units.
- Depreciation, marketing and administration costs behave as fixed costs.

The table on the next page shows the original budget and the actual costs.

Original Budget		Flexed Budget	Actual	Variance Fav (Adv)
30,000	Sales volume (units)		32,500	
£		£	£	£
840,000	Sales revenue		861,250	
	Costs:			
114,000	Materials		123,950	
165,000	Labour		170,320	
126,000	Distribution		131,200	
105,000	Energy		113,300	
50,000	Equipment hire		61,500	
83,400	Depreciation		82,300	
51,300	Marketing		55,350	
44,950	Administration		45,100	
739,650	Total costs		783,020	
100,350	Operating profit (loss)		78,230	

required

Complete the table, showing the flexed budget and variances.

solution

Original Budget		Flexed Budget	Actual	Variance Fav (Adv)
30,000	Sales volume (units)		32,500	
£		£	£	£
840,000	Sales revenue	910,000	861,250	(48,750)
	Costs:			
114,000	Materials	123,500	123,950	(450)
165,000	Labour	178,750	170,320	8,430
126,000	Distribution	136,500	131,200	5,300
105,000	Energy	112,500	113,300	(800)
50,000	Equipment hire	55,000	61,500	(6,500)
83,400	Depreciation	83,400	82,300	1,100
51,300	Marketing	51,300	55,350	(4,050)
44,950	Administration	44,950	45,100	(150)
739,650	Total costs	785,900	783,020	2,880
100,350	Operating profit (loss)	124,100	78,230	(45,870)

Flexed Budget Workings:

Sales revenue   (£840,000 / 30,000) x 32,500 = £910,000

Materials   (£114,000 / 30,000) x 32,500 = £123,500

Labour   (£165,000 / 30,000) x 32,500 = £178,750

Distribution   (£126,000 / 30,000) x 32,500 = £136,500

Energy   Fixed element: £105,000 – (30,000 x £3) = £15,000

                 Total flexed cost: £15,000 + (32,500 x £3) = £112,500

Equipment hire   Cost per step: £50,000 / 10 = £5,000

                 Number new of steps is 11 (up to 33,000 units) 11 x £5,000 = £55,000

Depreciation, marketing and administration costs are unchanged.

flexible budgets in marginal costing format

The format of marginal costing operating statements is shown in Chapter 1. As flexible budgets involve separating the fixed and variable parts of costs, they can easily be shown in marginal costing format if required. The variable costs are listed first (including variable overheads) and the fixed costs (which may include direct costs) are then grouped together. The Case Study that follows demonstrates this. The high-low method is not used because the information is given in a different way.

Case Study

TT LIMITED: MARGINAL COSTING

TT Ltd produces a single chemical product, TCH, which cannot be stored as work-in-progress or finished goods for technical reasons. For the year ended 31 August 20-3, the budget was for 10,000 litres of TCH to be produced and sold, but the actual production and sales for the period amounted to 11,000 litres. An operating results statement, with attached notes, is shown opposite.

Notes

1   There are no opening or closing work-in-progress or finished goods.

2   The cost of direct material is a variable cost.

3   The cost of direct production labour is a fixed cost, because the employees are paid a fixed wage. The employees available are sufficient to produce up to 12,000 litres of TCH.

4   The cost of power is semi-variable and the fixed part of the cost allowed for in the budget is £30,000. However, the fixed part of the actual cost is £27,660, due to re-negotiation of the contract with the power company.

TT Ltd Operating results for the year ended 31 August 20-3

	Budget		Actual	
Volume (litres of TCH)	10,000		11,000	
	£	£	£	£
Revenue		450,000		489,500
Direct costs:				
Material	80,000		90,200	
Production labour	95,000		98,000	
Power	46,500		45,700	
	221,500		233,900	
Fixed overheads	130,000		126,400	
Cost of sales		351,500		360,300
Operating profit		98,500		129,200

required

Calculate the following:

1 the budgeted unit selling price

2 the budgeted material cost per litre of TCH

3 the budgeted marginal cost (variable cost) of power

4 the actual marginal cost of power

5 prepare a marginal costing operating results statement, comparing the actual results with a flexible budget for 11,000 litres and showing the variances

6 explain briefly why the revised operating results statement is different from the original one, and state one advantage of flexible budgeting

solution

1 The budgeted unit selling price is £450,000 ÷ 10,000 = £45 per litre.

2 The budgeted material cost per litre is £80,000 ÷ 10,000 = £8.

3 The total budgeted cost of power is £46,500, of which £30,000 is fixed (note 4). Therefore the variable part of the cost is £16,500 for 10,000 litres.

The budgeted marginal cost of power is therefore £16,500 ÷ 10,000 = £1.65 per litre of TCH.

4 The total actual cost of power is £45,700, of which £27,660 is fixed. Therefore the actual marginal cost of power is £(45,700 − 27,660) ÷ 11,000 = £1.64 per litre of TCH.

5 The answer is shown in the following table, using the above answers to calculate the variable costs for 11,000 litres. Marginal costing format is used.

TT Ltd Flexible budgeting results statement for the year ended 31 August 20-3						
	Flexible budget		Actual results		Variance	
Litres of TCH	11,000		11,000		-	
	£	£	£	£	£	
Revenue **W1**		495,000		489,500	5,500	A
Marginal costs:						
Material **W2**	88,000		90,200		2,200	A
Power **W3**	18,150		18,040		110	F
Total marginal costs		106,150		108,240	2,090	A
Contribution		388,850		381,260	7,590	A
Fixed costs						
Direct Labour	95,000		98,000		3,000	A
Power **W4**	30,000		27,660		2,340	F
Overheads	130,000		126,400		3,600	F
Total fixed costs		255,000		252,060	2,940	F
Operating Profit		133,850		129,200	4,650	A

workings:

Note these use answers 1 to 4:

W1 Budget = £45 x 11,000 and actual is as given. (Note that the sales variance is Adverse when actual revenue is less than budget.)

W2 Budget = £8 x 11,000 and actual is as given.

W3 Budget = £1.65 x 11,000 and actual is £45,700 – £27,660 or £1.64 x 11,000.

W4 Fixed part of the power costs are as given. Fixed overheads are also given.

solution (continued)

6 The revised operating results statement is different from the original one because the costs have been separated into their fixed and variable parts. A flexed budget for 11,000 litres can then be prepared, to show what the results should have been for this level of output and sales. This is not the same as the original budget because the budgeted revenue and some of the budgeted costs depend on the number of litres. This is emphasised by the marginal costing layout. The budgeted profit is higher than the original one, because there are more litres of TCH to contribute to the fixed costs and profit.

The revised statement has the advantage that the comparison is more meaningful when we compare like with like, ie both budget and actual figures are applicable to 11,000 litres of TCH.

This report presents relevant, useful information in a clear format.

REASONS FOR VARIANCES

It is important that you can not only calculate and report variances accurately, but that you can also suggest possible reasons for variances. Recommended action will then follow logically from the reasons identified. You should always use the information provided when suggesting possible causes of actual results not being in line with a flexed budget, and not just learn an 'all-purpose' list.

However the following are some of the main categories that reasons for variances will fall into, and can be used as a starting point when analysing budget reports.

■ **poorly set budget**

If a budget is not set at an appropriate level, then variances are bound to occur. This can apply to both budgets that are too difficult to achieve (budgeted income set too high or budgeted costs set too low) and to budgets that are too easy. As discussed in Chapter 3, participation in budget setting can result in achievable budgets, but there is also a danger of managers setting themselves easy targets.

■ **inaccurate cost behaviour assumptions**

Where budgets have been flexed based on assumptions about cost behaviour that are inaccurate the result will also be cost variances. If, for example, a cost is believed to be fixed when it is really semi-variable then adverse variances will arise when the activity level increases.

■ **selling prices not in line with budget**

If the actual sales income is not in line with the flexed budget the variance must be caused by a difference in selling price. This is because any change in sales volume will have been accounted for when the budget was flexed. You should therefore take care not to suggest that sales volume is a possible cause.

■ **usage of materials or other costs**

Variances relating to material and other costs (for example labour or power costs) may be caused by the quantity used being different to what was expected. For example there may be materials wastage or labour inefficiency or more units of power used. This is a separate cause from the price per unit of these costs.

■ **price of materials or other costs**

This is the other possibility for the cause of cost variances. The price per unit of material (or rate per hour of labour etc) may differ from the amounts assumed in the budget. Cost variances may result from a combination of usage and price variances.

You will recall that one of the objectives of a budgetary system is so that management can exercise control over activities and costs. In order to exert control, it makes sense that management time is focussed on the more important variances. You will have come across the idea of 'significant' variances earlier in your studies. These are variances that are outside of a predetermined 'control limit' based on either a percentage of the budget or some absolute amount. These are where investigations should be carried out to establish the reasons for variances and what action should follow.

Remember that there may be some costs within budget areas that are not fully in the control of the budget holder. For example, if there was a change in depreciation policy that resulted in production depreciation exceeding the budget it would be unlikely that this was the responsibility of the Production Manager. Alternatively, if he had purchased equipment without authorisation and this created the additional depreciation then the Production Manager would be fully accountable. Care must therefore be taken to correctly establish the underlying causes of variances.

STANDARD COSTING

Standard costing was developed primarily in the manufacturing industry as a formal method for calculating the expected costs of products. It differs from general budget setting (which is normally concerned with the costs of sections of the organisation), because it focuses on the cost of what the organisation produces (the 'cost units').

Standard costing establishes in detail the standard cost of each component of a product, so that a total cost can be calculated for that product.

Standard costing is ideal for situations where components are identical and manufacturing operations are repetitive, and is often used alongside budgeting.

advantages of standard costing

The main advantages of operating with a standard costing system in place are that the standard costs can be used:

■ to help with **decision making**, for example as a basis for pricing decisions

■ to assist in **planning**, for example to plan the quantity and cost of the resources needed for future production

■ as a mechanism for **controlling** costs: the standard costs for the actual production can be compared with the actual costs incurred, and the differences (called 'variances') calculated. This is so that appropriate action can be taken

using standard costing

A standard costing system will be time consuming to set up initially, and will need to be kept updated if it is to be useful. It enables detailed costs to be built up which are also very useful for budgeting purposes.

For example, suppose the standard data for one unit of a particular product is as follows:

- direct materials are 5 kilos at £4.50 per kilo
- direct labour requirement is 2 hours at £12.00 per hour
- fixed overheads are absorbed at £13.00 per direct labour hour

A standard cost card would bring this data together as follows:

	Quantity of input	Cost per unit of input	Cost per unit produced
Direct material	5 kilos	£4.50	£22.50
Direct labour	2 hours	£12.00	£24.00
Fixed overheads	2 hours	£13.00	£26.00
Total standard cost			£72.50

This data could then easily be used to help create budgets. For example, if the plan was to produce 19,500 units in a period, then the direct material budget could be calculated simply as £22.50 x 19,500 units = £438,750.

analysing cost variances

Standard costing techniques can be used to divide cost variances into sub-variances relating to usage and price. The next section deals with the calculation of these variances. Standard costing is covered in detail in the unit 'Management Accounting: Decision and Control', but you also need to be able to calculate these variances to help understand the causes of cost variances when monitoring against budgets. Where standard costing is being used, the budgets will have been built up using standard costs, so the information required for the calculation of these variances should be available.

Using standard costing will enable us to analyse the cost variances calculated from the flexed budget. We can identify separately the variances caused by price and usage (for materials) and rate and efficiency (for labour). This will make it easier to correctly identify the causes of the variances.

DIRECT MATERIAL VARIANCES

The two variances that relate to the cost of materials are:

■ the direct material **price** variance

■ the direct material **usage** variance

The **price** variance measures how much of the difference between the expected and actual cost of materials is due to paying a **price** for materials that is different to the standard.

The direct material **usage** variance measures how much of the difference between the expected and actual cost of materials is due to **using a different quantity** of materials.

Together these two variances will account for the whole difference between the expected and actual cost of the materials.

direct material price variance

The direct material price variance =

the standard cost of the actual quantity of material used	*minus*	the actual cost of the actual quantity of material used

We are making a comparison between two values – the standard cost of the actual materials and the actual cost. Notice that both figures relate to the **actual materials used**, so that we are comparing two costs that both relate to the same actual quantity.

If the actual cost is less than the standard then the variance will be favourable; if it is more, the variance will be adverse.

If you carry out the calculation as outlined above, then a positive answer will be favourable and a negative one adverse.

direct material usage variance

The direct material usage variance =

the standard quantity of material for actual production at standard price	*minus*	the actual quantity of material used at standard price

With this usage variance we are also making a comparison between two values. This time the comparison is based on two quantities – the standard quantity for the actual production and the actual quantity used. These quantities are turned into values by costing them both at **standard price**.

remembering how to calculate direct variances

The key to calculating the variances accurately is remembering the basis of the formulas. One method that may help is the mnemonic 'PAUS', based on:

> **P**rice variances are based on
> **A**ctual quantities, but
> **U**sage variances are based on
> **S**tandard prices.

One explanation of why the variances are calculated in this way is that purchases are sometimes converted to standard price (and a price variance calculated) when the materials are bought. This price variance would relate to the actual materials bought. The materials in inventory would then be valued at standard price, and the usage variance would be calculated based on the amounts issued to production at standard price.

The two material variances that we have looked at will account for the whole of any difference between the standard cost of the material used for the actual production level and the actual cost. This amount is known as the total direct material variance (or material cost variance), and is the variance originally calculated by comparing the flexed budget with the actual costs.

DIRECT LABOUR VARIANCES

The approach for calculating direct labour variances is very similar to direct material variances.

The two variances that relate to the cost of labour are:

- the **direct labour rate variance**
- the **direct labour efficiency variance**

The direct labour rate variance measures the labour cost difference due to the rate paid, and the direct labour efficiency variance measures the cost difference due to the amount of labour time used. The concept of labour 'rate' is similar to material 'price', and labour 'efficiency' is similar to material 'usage', as explained below. This makes remembering the calculation method and interpreting the variances much easier.

direct labour rate variance

The direct labour rate variance =

the standard cost of the actual labour hours used	*minus*	the actual cost of the actual labour hours used

We are again making a comparison between two values – the standard cost of the actual labour hours and the actual cost. Just like the material price variance, the labour rate variance is comparing two figures that both relate to an actual quantity – here the actual quantity is the **actual number of labour hours**.

direct labour efficiency variance

The direct labour efficiency variance =

standard labour hours for actual production at standard rate	*minus*	actual labour hours used at standard rate

This also has a strong resemblance to the material usage variance; we are simply considering the quantity of labour hours instead of the quantity of material.

Just like the material usage variance, we are using a standard figure to value these two quantities – this time it is the standard labour rate that is used. Although this variance is all about comparison of two amounts of time, we must remember to convert the answer into an amount of money by valuing the hours at the standard rate.

Provided we can remember the similarity of the labour variances to the material ones, there is probably no need to use any other memory aid. The direct labour variances must add up to the total difference in labour cost between the flexed budget costs and the actual costs (the labour cost variance).

We will now illustrate how these variances can be calculated.

| | | | Case Study |

MONITOR LIMITED:
STANDARD COSTING VARIANCES

Monitor Limited is a manufacturing company. An operating statement has already been prepared, based on the actual sales volume of 600 units, as follows:

Number of units produced and sold	600	600		
	Budget £	Actual £	Variance £	Adverse or Favourable
Sales Revenue	300,000	295,000	5,000	Adverse
Direct Materials	48,000	49,200	1,200	Adverse
Direct Labour	60,000	65,800	5,800	Adverse
Production Overheads	74,200	73,600	600	Favourable
Administration Overheads	35,900	36,000	100	Adverse
Selling and Distribution Overheads	28,400	25,300	3,100	Favourable
Operating Profit	53,500	45,100	8,400	Adverse

The company uses standard costing to develop its budgets, and the standard direct material and direct labour costs for one unit are as follows:

Direct Materials   10 kilograms at £8.00 per kilogram = £80.00
Direct Labour   8 hours at £12.50 per hour = £100.00

You have established that 6,350 kilograms of material was actually used, and that there were 4,700 direct labour hours utilised.

required

(a)   Calculate the following variances:
       Direct material price variance
       Direct material usage variance
       Direct labour rate variance
       Direct labour efficiency variance

(b)   Comment briefly on the information that these variances have provided.

solution

(a) **Direct material price variance**

Standard cost of actual quantity of material used	minus	Actual cost of the actual quantity of material used
(6,350 kilograms x £8.00)	–	£49,200

= £1,600 Favourable

Direct material usage variance

Standard quantity of material for actual production at standard price	minus	Actual quantity of material used at standard price
(600 units x 10 kilograms x £8.00)	–	(6,350 x £8.00)

= £2,800 Adverse

Direct labour rate variance

Standard cost of actual labour hours used	minus	Actual cost of the actual labour hours used
(4,700 hours x £12.50)	–	£65,800

= £7,050 Adverse

Direct labour efficiency variance

Standard labour hours for actual production at standard rate	minus	Actual labour hours used at standard rate
(600 units x 8 hours x £12.50)	–	(4,700 hours x £12.50)

= £1,250 Favourable

(b) The adverse variance related to direct material cost of £1,200 (from the operating statement) is made up of a price variance of £1,600 favourable, and a usage variance of £2,800 adverse. This means that while the material was purchased for a lower price than standard, the saving was more than offset by using more material than planned. Further investigation would be needed to determine the causes of these variances.

The adverse direct labour cost variance of £5,800 shown in the operating statement can be analysed into a rate variance of £7,050 adverse and an efficiency variance of £1,250 favourable. This shows that the rate paid was greater than standard (an average rate of £65,800 / 4,700 hours = £14 per hour). However the time taken was less than standard, and this made some savings. Again, further investigation would be needed to determine the reasons for these variances.

Note that in the Case Study used here the actual activity level was already identical to the budget. If that had not been the case, usually a flexed budget would have been prepared, and the sub-variances calculated from that data.

OTHER PERFORMANCE INDICATORS

So far in this chapter we have examined the use of variances – the differences between actual performance and the budget (which is usually flexed). While this is a major tool for monitoring performance, there are also other performance indicators that can be used.

Many of these performance indicators can be used in two distinct ways:

■ at the budget preparation stage to ensure that the budget (if achieved) will produce the required level of performance (as we saw in Chapter 4), and

■ at the monitoring stage to analyse the impact of the actual performance

Suitable performance indicators can be considered in four groups, which are shown here, with examples:

■ standard costing data

      quantity of material per unit

      cost of material per kilogram or metre etc

      labour time per unit

      labour rate per hour

■ financial measures

      gross profit margin (or %)

      net profit margin (or %)

      average selling price

      cost per unit of production

■ physical measures

      machine utilisation ratios (a measure of capacity)

      material wastage rate (a measure of efficiency)

      idle time level (a measure of efficiency)

      reject rate (a measure of quality)

■ qualitative data

      customer satisfaction

      employee satisfaction

TUFFWUN LIMITED:
PERFORMANCE INDICATORS

situation

Tuffwun Limited is a manufacturing company. It does not currently use standard costing. The following report has already been produced, comparing the actual results with a flexed budget. The original fixed budget assumed production and sales of 40,000 units. The actual sales were 35,000 units.

Flexible Budget Operating Statement (35,000 units)

	Budget £	Actual £	Variances £
Sales	525,000	560,000	35,000 F
less variable costs:			
materials	157,500	159,250	1,750 A
labour	122,500	133,000	10,500 A
production overheads	35,000	35,000	0
Contribution	210,000	232,750	22,750 F
less fixed costs:			
production overheads	50,000	61,050	11,050 A
admin and sales overheads	50,000	51,000	1,000 A
Operating Profit	110,000	120,700	10,700 F

required

(a)   Explain briefly the reason for the sales variance.

(b)   Suggest and calculate suitable performance indicators that could be used to evaluate sales level and profitability based on the information provided.

solution

(a)   Since the operating statement is based on the same sales volume for both flexed budget and actual figures, the favourable sales budget must be due to selling prices. We can calculate that the actual selling prices are an average of £16 per unit, but the budgeted selling price was £15 per unit.

(b)   The following are possible performance indicators (with workings):

Performance Indicator	Budget	Actual
Actual sales units as % of original budget	N/A	35,000 / 40,000 % = 87.5%
Variable costs as % of sales	£315,000 / £525,000 % = 60%	£327,250 / £560,000 % = 58.4%
Contribution as % of sales	£210,000 / £525,000 % = 40%	£232,750 / £560,000 % = 41.6%
Operating profit as % of sales	£110,000 / £525,000 % = 21%	£120,700 / £560,000 % = 21.6%

MOTIVATIONAL ASPECTS OF BUDGETS

The budget is not usually designed specifically to motivate employees, but the process of budgeting and the budget itself can affect the behaviour of employees. The effect may be to motivate or to demotivate under different circumstances.

A budget will help to motivate employees if they accept that it is achievable. If it is too easy to achieve, it will not be sufficient motivation, and if it is too difficult it will not be accepted. If a budget which employees see as impossible is imposed upon them, they may be demotivated to the extent of setting out to prove that the budget is wrong, which would lead to completely the opposite effect than that which is intended.

There have been a number of research projects carried out to investigate the effects of budgeting on people's behaviour, and to a certain extent the results appear to give conflicting views. However, there seems to be general agreement that employees are motivated to work towards a target or budget:

■ only if they accept it as their personal goal
■ if the target is high enough to be a challenge
■ if, although it is a challenge, they see it as achievable

Some research has looked at the effect of involving people in the budget setting process (participation), to see whether this results in a greater likelihood of the budget being accepted in this way.

participation in budget preparation

A participative budget system means that those who will have to work to a particular budget are involved in its preparation. They are consulted throughout the process, so that they can input their specialised knowledge of the work involved and contribute to the planning process involved in budgeting. This is sometimes described as a 'bottom up' style of budgeting, as opposed to 'top down', which would refer to the situation where the budget is imposed on people by higher levels of management.

The main advantages of the method of participative budgeting are:

- the budget takes account of information from those with specialised knowledge
- those involved will have improved awareness of organisational goals
- those involved will accept the budget and be motivated to work to it
- coordination and cooperation between those involved will improve
- participating in budget preparation broadens their experience and develops new skills
- participation in budget setting gives those involved a more positive attitude towards the organisation and this leads to better performance

It should be borne in mind, however, that these advantages depend on the participation being genuine: if people are consulted, but their opinions later appear to be ignored, the effects will be the opposite of those listed above. (This is sometimes referred to as 'pseudo-participation'.)

Supporters of the idea of participation in budgeting may point to apparent improvements in performance as 'proof' of its motivating effect. It should be borne in mind that coincidences can occur, and the improvement may have happened for some other reason: favourable cost variances can result from suppliers reducing their prices, for example, or sales volumes might increase because of purely external factors like changes in the weather.

Another reason for favourable results may be the introduction of **budgetary slack**. This means that managers have succeeded in obtaining a budget based on an over-estimation of costs or an under-estimation of income. They are then more likely to be able to achieve a good level of performance when measured against the budget. An argument against participation could be that it increases the risk of managers being able to introduce budgetary slack.

Research projects relating to participation in budgeting do not seem to have provided any firm conclusions about its motivational effects. It is not surprising that the effects seem to depend on the attitudes of the individuals involved, and different people react in different ways. Some employees may not want to spend time on budgeting, or may feel they do not have the necessary skills, so that participation would be seen as added pressure on them rather than an opportunity. They may feel that it is not part of their job, or that they have not been trained to carry out the task. Therefore, under some circumstances, an imposed ('top down') method of budgeting may be preferred.

Imposing a budget is also likely to be quicker than a consultation process, and sometimes the timescale will mean that a participative approach is impossible. Managers must be able to respond quickly to changing circumstances and maintain the progress of their organisation in the required direction. Part of this response may be to revise budgets at short notice.

performance related pay

Performance related pay is a method of rewarding employees in the form of bonuses, options to buy shares or other incentives, with a view to motivating them to improve their own performance or, in the case of managers, the performance of the part of the organisation which they manage.

Our earlier discussions of authority, responsibility and motivation are all relevant here. The principles of performance measurement are also relevant, as no scheme for performance related pay would be possible without some way of measuring performance. There must be some standard or target against which to measure the actual results, and this is most likely to be in the form of a budget.

Taking all these aspects into account, the conditions necessary for performance related pay to be an effective way of motivating people can be summarised as follows. Those involved will need:

- to understand the organisational goals
- to want to work towards achieving those goals
- to have budgets which they accept as consistent with achieving those goals
- to feel that the budgets are challenging, but achievable
- to have the appropriate skills to achieve improved performance
- to feel that they can influence the performance outcomes
- to see the measurement of performance outcomes as fair
- to be motivated by the level and type of rewards in the scheme

The scheme itself must have:

- clear definitions as to what performance outcomes will be rewarded
- an organisational structure which allows performance to be linked to authority and responsibility
- a method for measuring the relevant performance outcomes
- information systems which collect the data necessary to measure these outcomes

■ rewards for improved performance which are at a suitable level and of a type which will motivate employees

goal congruence

We have seen earlier that the overall goals of the organisation have to be translated into subsidiary goals for parts of the organisation and then, through budgetary planning and control, the organisation should make progress towards its goals. This describes the ideal situation, but the complexities of these processes and the effects on the behaviour of individuals within the organisation may mean that the ideal is not achieved.

In practice, when we look at a particular department, for example, we may find that its manager has different goals, which are not actually in line with those of the whole. Typical examples are sometimes described as 'empire-building' – increasing production of one product for example, or employing more staff, or alternatively cutting costs to achieve favourable variances. These strategies to enhance the manager's own situation and performance may not be in the best interests of the organisation as a whole, and may be contrary to its stated goals. This is called **dysfunctional** decision making or behaviour.

The term 'goal congruence' is used if the ideal situation does exist, and the goals of parts of the organisation are in line with those of the whole. The complex process of breaking down the long-term goals of the whole organisation into shorter-term aims for its parts may have involved negotiation and compromise. These planning and budgeting activities are never 'finished', as information is continuously fed back and fed forward so that action can be taken to steer the organisation in the required direction. To keep the organisation on track, a well designed budgetary control system, which leads to goal congruence, is a very important factor.

Effective participation in budgeting does require ethical behaviour from all involved. Activities by participants such as building in budgetary slack and empire building may be considered unethical, as would be the management carrying out 'pseudo participation' practices as outlined earlier.

conflict between budget priorities

We introduced the purposes of budgeting earlier in this book. Some organisations will view these purposes differently to others. It may be that control is the most important aspect of budgeting for one organisation, but for another, using budgeting to produce motivational targets may be the highest priority.

It will be impossible for all the diverse purposes of budgeting to be equally well served by a budgeting system, and conflict can arise. For example, where a budget is used primarily for cost control then this can stifle expansion of the organisation. Alternatively, if a budget's main aim is to provide a challenging target, the budget is unlikely to be consistently achieved. This will mean that the use of the budget for planning purposes will be restricted.

MANAGEMENT ACTION

As part of the process for monitoring and control, there must be a stage involving some management action as a result of the monitoring. If there is no action, then the monitoring could be seen as a waste of time!

Actions are either to:

- change the current situation to improve the 'actual' figures in future
- acknowledge that the budget needs to be altered for the future
- or a combination of these

feedback

Feedback is information obtained and reported after comparing the budgeted and actual results for a control period.

Feedback is used to determine the necessary control action if results are significantly different from the budget. What is meant by 'significantly different'? This would have to be decided in advance. It could be defined in terms of absolute amounts or percentages of the budget, that is, 'control limits' would be set.

Only when the feedback shows variances going beyond the control limits would they be reported for action to be taken by the appropriate person. This is called 'exception reporting', which has the advantage that only the 'significant' differences are brought to the attention of management, thus saving time and avoiding the risk of important figures being lost among a mass of data.

favourable variances

It is often thought that only adverse variances are significant, but **favourable** variances which are **beyond the control limits** are equally important and may require action to be taken.

The word 'favourable' is perhaps misleading because it suggests something good. Favourable variances may indeed indicate some advantageous situation which it would be useful to investigate to see if it can be continued, for example efficiency improvements. However, large favourable variances may not be desirable in some cases, for example favourable materials variances may result from using the wrong material or using insufficient material to maintain the quality of a product.

control action

The control action to be taken on receipt of feedback from the monitoring of budgets depends on the situation.

If the reason for the variance can be identified it may be possible to correct it, in order to bring the actual results for the next control period back in line with (or at least closer to) the budget. The **feedback loop** is shown in the diagram on the next page. The feedback loop is an important part of the Budgetary Control process.

Sometimes it is not possible to bring the actual results back in line with the budget, because there has been a permanent change in costs which is not controllable by the managers of the organisation. This could be due to external factors, such as national wage agreements or permanent price changes (increases or reductions). The action to be taken then involves adjusting the budget to plan for realistic costs, so that the feedback from the next control period is more meaningful. This brings us to the idea of feeding forward information.

feedforward

Feedforward is information about the current performance of an organisation and its environment which is used in budgeting for the future.

The budgeting process starts from identifying the organisation's objectives and translating these into desired results for the budget period. For example, if the long-term objective is to achieve a particular level of market share, the short-term aim can be expressed in terms of budgeted sales volume.

In a feedforward system, the initial budget is considered by looking at the results it is expected to achieve in comparison with the desired results. This process uses information about the current performance of the organisation (feedback) and information about the economic environment, together with the budget.

If the results, according to the budget, are significantly different from the desired results, then the budget may be amended to eliminate the differences. However, the organisation's aims and objectives may have to be re-considered and brought closer to what is achievable. In either case, a revised budget and/or revised objectives should help to ensure that future results do meet the organisation's objectives.

The feedforward loop is shown on the diagram on the next page. Notice that the feedforward loop takes information to the Budgetary Planning process for the *next* period.

This whole process provides a cycle of continuous improvement. When rolling budgets are used the cycle may even be repeated on a monthly basis, as information on actual performance is used to revise budgets.

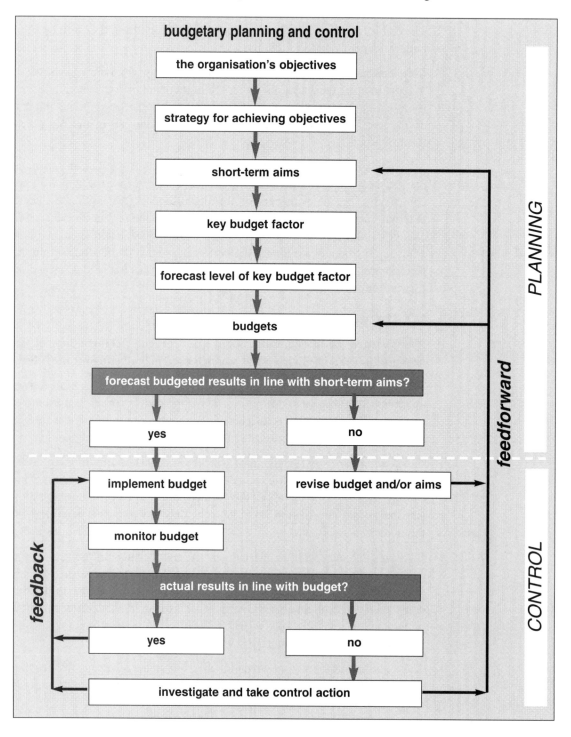

Case Study

FLEXIE LIMITED:
MONITORING PERFORMANCE

The original March budget for Flexie Limited assumed sales of 30,000 units. The actual sales were 32,500 units. The following assumptions were made about the behaviour of the costs:

- Materials, labour and distribution costs are variable.
- Energy costs are semi-variable.
- Equipment hire is a stepped cost.
- Depreciation, marketing and administration costs behave as fixed costs.

Following the actual performance, the following additional information has been obtained:

- The actual labour rate paid was in line with the budgeted rate.
- The Distribution Manager had negotiated a new long-term contract with the transport contractor at reduced rates.
- The hire company normally used for equipment hire has closed and a more expensive company had to be used.
- A planned advertising campaign had been brought forward to this period.

The flexed budget and variances have been calculated and are shown below.

Original Budget		Flexed Budget	Actual	Variance Fav (Adv)
30,000	Sales volume (units)		32,500	
£		£	£	£
840,000	Sales revenue	910,000	861,250	(48,750)
	Costs:			
114,000	Materials	123,500	123,950	(450)
165,000	Labour	178,750	170,320	8,430
126,000	Distribution	136,500	131,200	5,300
105,000	Energy	112,500	113,300	(800)
50,000	Equipment hire	55,000	61,500	(6,500)
83,400	Depreciation	83,400	82,300	1,100
51,300	Marketing	51,300	55,350	(4,050)
44,950	Administration	44,950	45,100	(150)
739,650	Total costs	785,900	783,020	2,880
100,350	Operating profit (loss)	124,100	78,230	(45,870)

required

Review the information provided and write an email to the chief executive which explains:

- Why there is an adverse sales revenue variance despite achieving a sales level in excess of the original budget.
- Possible causes for each of the cost variances which exceed the control level of £4,000.
- How using a rolling budget could improve accuracy of budgeting for this organisation.

solution

Email	
To	Chief Executive
From	Budget Accountant
Subject	March Budget Review

Sales Revenue Variance

The variance is calculated by comparing the flexed budget with the actual sales revenue. This means that both the figures are based on the actual activity level of 32,500 units. The budgeted average selling price was £28 per unit, but the actual average selling price was £26.50. It is this price difference that accounts for the adverse variance of £48,750. It is likely that this unbudgeted price reduction was a factor in increased sales levels.

Possible Causes for Cost Variances

The following are possible causes for the cost variances that exceed the control level of £4,000:

- Labour £8,430 favourable

  Since the actual rate of pay is the same as the budgeted amount, the cause of this variance must lie elsewhere. There are two possibilities:

  - The working could be more efficient than expected, so that fewer hours are taken than planned.
  - The assumption that labour cost behaves entirely as a variable cost could be incorrect. The actual cost of labour is greater than that shown in the original budget (which was based on a lower activity level), so if there was a fixed element to the cost behaviour this could account for the favourable variance.

- Distribution £5,300 favourable

  It seems likely that the reduced rates payable on the long-term transport contract are the cause of the lower than expected distribution costs.

- Equipment Hire £6,500 adverse

  The closure of the usual hire company and the use of a more expensive alternative seems to be the likely cause of this variance.

- Marketing £4,050 adverse

  The earlier than expected advertising campaign seems to be the likely cause of this variance. The campaign may also be partly responsible for the higher than expected sales level (along with the average selling price reduction).

Rolling Budgets

Rolling budgets can increase the speed with which an organisation goes through the budgeting cycle. In particular it can improve responsiveness to changing conditions by feeding forward new information by revising part of the existing budget instead of waiting for a whole new budgeting period. Issues like the reduced average selling price (if to be continued), the revised transport contract and the implications of the closure of the equipment hire company could be fed into the budget for the next month or quarter, rather than waiting for the next year's budget.

Chapter Summary	
	▣ For budgeting, it is important to have information about how costs behave in relation to levels of activity. This is particularly relevant to the preparation of flexible budgets. A fixed budget is one which is prepared for a specific level of activity, whereas a flexed or flexible budget is one which allows for a change in the level of activity.
	▣ After splitting all the costs into their fixed and variable parts, a flexible budget can be prepared by calculating the costs and income at the required level of activity.
	▣ Standard costing involves establishing expected costs for each element of a cost unit. It can be used alongside budgeting and will enable more detailed analysis of variances.
	▣ Budgets are most likely to have a motivational effect on employees if they are seen to be challenging but achievable.
	▣ Participation in the budgeting process by those to whom the budget will apply may increase the likelihood of their acceptance of the budget.

Key Terms		
	fixed budget	a budget which is set for a particular level of activity
	flexed (or flexible) budget	a budget which is adjusted to allow for changes in costs (and income) resulting from a change in the level of activity
	relevant range	the range of levels of activity within which a certain pattern of cost behaviour applies
	standard costing	the establishment in detail of the standard cost of each component of a product so that a total cost can be calculated for the product. This also allows detailed variances to be calculated when compared with actual costs

material price variance	the part of the material cost variance that is due to the price of material differing from standard
material usage variance	the part of the material cost variance that is due to the quantity of material used differing from standard
labour rate variance	the part of the labour cost variance that is due to the labour rate differing from standard
labour efficiency variance	the part of the labour cost variance that is due to the number of labour hours used differing from standard
participation in budgeting	a system of budgeting where managers of budget centres and others are consulted and involved in the preparation of budgets
budgetary slack	an additional allowance within a budget that has been obtained by over-estimating costs or under-estimating income in order to make favourable variances easier to achieve
performance related pay	a system of financially rewarding managers or other employees based on their (or their department's) performance when measured against a budget or other benchmark
goal congruence	the situation in which the goals of individuals within an organisation are in line with the goals of the whole organisation
dysfunctional behaviour	behaviour or decision making by individuals within an organisation which is in their own interests, but not in line with the goals of the whole organisation
budget period	the period of time for which a budget is prepared
control period	the part of a budget period after which budgeted and actual results are compared
feedback	information obtained and reported after comparing the budgeted and actual results for a control period – feedback is used to determine necessary control action if results show significant differences from the budget
feedforward	information about the current performance of an organisation and its environment which is used in budgeting for the future – a feedforward system attempts to ensure that future results will meet the organisation's objectives

Activities

6.1 A monthly operating statement is shown below with some explanatory notes. You are required to flex the budget, calculate variances and show whether each variance is favourable or adverse.

Monthly Operating Statement

	Budget	Actual
Volume	31,500	34,000
	£	£
Revenue	2,520,000	2,856,000
Costs		
Material	441,000	510,000
Labour	567,000	616,250
Distribution	6,300	7,000
Energy	151,000	164,000
Equipment hire	32,000	35,000
Depreciation	182,000	180,000
Marketing	231,000	235,000
Administration	186,000	189,000
Total	1,796,300	1,936,250
Operating Profit	723,700	919,750

Monthly Operating Statement

Volume 34,000

	Flexed Budget £	Actual £	Variance Fav/(Adv) £
Revenue		2,856,000	
Costs			
Material		510,000	
Labour		616,250	
Distribution		7,000	
Energy		164,000	
Equipment hire		35,000	
Depreciation		180,000	
Marketing		235,000	
Administration		189,000	
Total		1,936,250	
Operating Profit		919,750	

Notes

Material, labour and distribution costs are variable.

The budget for energy is semi-variable. The variable element is £4.00 per unit.

The budget for equipment hire is stepped, increasing at every 4,000 units of monthly production.

Depreciation, marketing and administration costs are fixed.

6.2   The following table shows the original budget and the actual costs for a period.

Original Budget		Flexed Budget	Actual	Variance Fav (Adv)
60,000	Sales volume (units)		57,300	
£		£	£	£
960,000	Sales revenue		945,250	
	Costs:			
138,000	Materials		134,950	
234,000	Labour		222,390	
72,000	Distribution		70,400	
85,000	Energy		82,350	
88,000	Equipment hire		86,950	
91,400	Depreciation		92,300	
59,600	Marketing		65,300	
66,500	Administration		65,250	
834,500	Total costs		819,890	
125,500	Operating profit (loss)		125,360	

Notes:

Materials, labour and distribution costs are variable.

Energy costs are semi-variable. The variable element is £0.50 per unit.

Equipment hire is a stepped cost. Each step is based on up to 8,000 units.

Depreciation, marketing and administration costs behave as fixed costs.

Required:

Complete the table, showing the flexed budget and variances.

6.3   You are asked to review the Operating Statement shown below, and the background information provided, and to make recommendations.

Operating Statement for May 20-9			
		Sales (units)	1,360,000
	Budget	Actual	Variance Fav/(Adverse)
	£	£	£
Revenue	2,720,000	2,992,000	272,000
Variable Costs			
Material	816,000	884,000	(68,000)
Labour	612,000	571,200	40,800
Distribution	108,800	111,100	(2,300)
Power	136,000	138,000	(2,000)
Equipment hire	68,000	67,500	500
	1,740,800	1,771,800	(31,000)
Contribution	979,200	1,220,200	241,000
Fixed costs			
Power	14,000	15,000	(1,000)
Equipment hire	10,000	9,000	1,000
Depreciation	108,000	110,000	(2,000)
Marketing	121,000	128,000	(7,000)
Administration	147,000	151,000	(4,000)
	400,000	413,000	(13,000)
Operating Profit	579,200	807,200	228,000

The budget has been flexed to the actual number of units produced and sold. The original budget had been drawn up by the Chief Executive and communicated to senior managers by email.

Despite an unbudgeted price increase, the volume of units sold was higher than expected in the original budget. This seems to have been due to a very successful advertising campaign. Temporary staff had been recruited to avoid overtime costs.

One of the component parts of the product is made from brass which increased in price by 6% for part of the month.

Although pleased with the overall results, the Chief Executive is concerned that costs were above budget and has asked you to advise how control can be improved.

Write an email to the Chief Executive in which you:

(a)   Suggest possible reasons for the variances on materials, labour, marketing and administration.

(b)   Make recommendations on how cost accountability could be improved when setting budgets.

6.4 The standard cost data for one unit of Beta is as follows:

Materials   5 kilos at £10.60 per kilo

Labour   30 minutes at £16.00 per hour

During April, 1,530 units of Beta were produced.

The actual inputs were:

7,500 kilos material costing £82,500

780 hours labour costing £12,558

Required:

· Calculate the flexed budget, actual costs and total variances for materials and labour for April.

· Calculate the material price variance, the material usage variance, the labour rate variance and the labour efficiency variance for April.

6.5 The following data relating to materials and labour has been extracted from a fixed budget and actual figures.

	Budget	**Actual**
Units Produced	23,000	21,000
Material	£69,000	£65,000
Labour	£41,400	£42,000

The budgeted costs were built up from standard data for one unit as follows:

Material   1.5 metres at £2.00 per metre   £3.00

Labour   6 minutes at £18.00 per hour   £1.80

The actual quantity of material used was 31,550 metres.

The labour force worked for 2,800 hours.

Required:

(a) Prepare an extract from an operating statement showing flexed budget, actual costs and variances for materials and labour.

(b) Calculate material variances for price and usage, and labour variances for rate and efficiency.

(c) State which of the following statements are correct in relation to the information that you have prepared:

(a) The adverse material cost variance was mainly caused by high usage, with higher cost than standard being a contributory factor.

(b) The adverse material cost variance was mainly caused by high material prices, with higher usage than standard being a contributory factor.

(c)   The adverse material cost variance was caused by high prices, but this was offset by a favourable usage variance.

(d)   The significant labour cost variance was caused by paying higher rate per hour than standard. This was offset by taking less time than standard to complete the work.

(e)   The significant labour cost variance was caused by the labour force working more slowly than standard. This was offset by paying a lower than standard rate per hour.

(f)   The adverse labour cost variance is insignificant. The cost of the additional time taken is almost exactly matched by the savings from the lower pay rate.

6.6   Consider the following situation:

Peter Ltd makes and sells a single product, Product P. Peter Ltd uses absorption costing.

The budgeted variable cost of Product P is £5.00 per unit.

The budgeted full cost of Product P is £6.00 per unit, based on absorbing £1,000 per month of fixed production overheads into production of 1,000 units of P. (Non-production overheads budgeted at £1,750 per month are not absorbed.)

The original budget for Product P for November 20-3 was for 1,000 units to be produced and sold, opening and closing inventory of finished goods and work-in-progress being zero.

The actual results for November were that 800 units of P were sold and 1,000 were produced. The absorption costing budget and actual results for November 20-3 are shown below:

	Budget		Actual	
	£	£	£	£
Sales 1,000 x £10		10,000		
Sales 800 x £11				8,800
Opening inventory	-		-	
Cost of Production	6,000		6,000	
Less: closing inventory	-		1,200	
Cost of sales		6,000		4,800
Gross Profit		4,000		4,000
Non-production overheads		1,750		1,650
Net profit		2,250		2,350

Required:

Referring to the budgeted and actual results for November 20-3 shown above, give two reasons why the additional net profit of £100 does not necessarily give a fair indication of management performance in Peter Ltd in November 20-3. Explain briefly how the performance report could be improved.

6.7   The Excelsior Hotel is managed using a series of responsibility centres. Each responsibility centre has a manager who is accountable for its performance compared to budget. The budgets are prepared and issued by the General Manager.

The swimming pool is a cost centre, since hotel guests are not charged for use of the pool. The majority of costs do not depend on the number of guests who use the pool. The Pool Manager usually manages to remain within the fixed budget.

The hotel café is a profit centre, and is open to residents who are charged separately for their refreshments. Staff costs and food and drink costs vary according to how busy the café is. The Café Manager's performance when measured against his fixed budget varies considerably.

The General Manger is concerned that the Café Manager's performance is inconsistent, even though the Pool Manager is able to keep within budget. He wants to know whether the current budgeting system is motivating his managers, and whether the introduction of performance related pay would help.

Required:

Draft an email to the General Manager answering his questions.

Answers to chapter activities

CHAPTER 1: MANAGEMENT ACCOUNTING TECHNIQUES

1.1 Absorption cost per unit: (b)

(£240,000 + £180,000 + £600,000) / 48,000 = £21.25.

(Only production costs are included)

Marginal cost per unit: (a)

(£240,000 + £180,000) / 48,000 = £8.75

(Only variable costs are included)

1.2 (a) (1) **Profit Statements Using Absorption Costing**

	Week 1		Week 2	
	£	£	£	£
Sales		24,000		40,000
Less cost of sales:				
Opening Inventory	–		5,000	
Cost of Production:				
Direct Materials	5,000		5,000	
Direct Labour	9,000		9,000	
Fixed Overheads	6,000		6,000	
Less				
Closing Inventory	(5,000)		–	
		15,000		25,000
Profit		9,000		15,000

(2) **Profit Statements Using Marginal Costing**

	Week 1		Week 2	
	£	£	£	£
Sales		24,000		40,000
Less cost of sales:				
Opening Inventory	–		3,500	
Variable Cost of				
Production:	14,000		14,000	
Less Closing Inventory	(3,500)		–	
		10,500		17,500
Contribution		13,500		22,500
Less Fixed Costs		6,000		6,000
Profit		7,500		16,500

(b) The inventory valuation using absorption costing includes £6,000 ÷ 4,000 units = £1.50 per unit of fixed overheads, which is not included when using marginal costing. This means that the inventory of 1,000 units at the end of week one is valued at £1,500 more using absorption costing, and the profit recorded in week one is also £1,500 more. Marginal costing records a profit higher by £1,500 in week two, as the inventory falls by 1,000 units. Both systems show identical profits for the two weeks added together because the inventory level at the start of week one is the same as at the end of week two.

1.3 Based on the information given, activity based costing would appear to be most appropriate for the Radical Company. It is the only system that would cope with accurately costing the range of products outlined. For example, the developments and design costs for items that are constantly updated are likely to be greater than those with unchanged specifications. Similarly, the size of batches and lengths of production runs would have a cost impact that only ABC would recognise.

1.4

Situation	Suggested Accounting Treatment
Holiday pay for production workers	Charge to production in a labour hour overhead rate
Material wastage in production	Direct cost
Cost of the purchasing department	Activity based charge to production cost centres
Administrative wages	Allocate to administrative overheads
Computing services	Allocate to administrative overheads
Production equipment maintenance	Charge to production in a machine hour overhead rate
Depreciation of production equipment	Charge to production in a machine hour overhead rate
Redecoration of the sales showroom	Allocate to marketing overheads

1.5 Overhead recovery should be based on **Labour hours**.

The recovery rate will be **£2.00** per **labour hour**.

Working: £75,000 / 37,500 hours = £2.00

The process is labour intensive with only minor machine-based costs and time.

1.6 **(a)** Variable cost per unit = £(59,000 − 43,000) ÷ (110,000 − 70,000) = £0.40

Fixed cost = £43,000 − (£0.40 x 70,000) = £15,000

(b) Total cost for 80,000 units = £15,000 + (£0.40 x 80,000) = £47,000

1.7

Month	Budgeted Output (Units)	Budgeted Hire Costs
1	6,000	£1,200
2	8,000	£1,200
3	4,500	£600
4	9,000	£1,200
5	11,000	£1,800

CHAPTER 2: FORECASTING TECHNIQUES

2.1   Inflation trends in UK   Office for National Statistics

Value Added Tax (VAT) rates   HMRC website

Future production levels   Production Schedules

Demand for our products   Market Research

2.2   **(a)**   (e)   All the factors mentioned will influence the reliability of a forecast based on sampling.

(b)   (b) and (c) Historical trends in price changes can only be valid in the future if the trend is considered likely to continue. The reliability of the data will be improved by choosing as specific an index as possible.

(c)   (c)   Since maturity should be a relatively stable period it may provide the data for a sound forecast. However the fact that it will be followed at some point by a period of decline should not be ignored.

2.3   **(a)**   Average trend movement is difference between last and first trend figures, divided by number of movements.

= (6,290 − 5,800) ÷ 7 = +70

(b)   If trend is increasing at an average 70 policies per quarter, then by

Year 3 quarter 3 it will be 6,290 + (3 x 70)   = 6,500, and by

Year 3 quarter 4 it will be 6,290 + (4 x 70)   = 6,570

Adjusting these figures by the seasonal variations (which were identical for both years) gives:

Year 3 quarter 3 forecast of (6,500 + 880)   = 7,380

Year 3 quarter 4 forecast of (6,570 − 100)   = 6,470

2.4   **(a)**   Year 3:

Qtr 1   Sales Trend   =   (9 x £1,200) + £83,000   = £93,800

Qtr 2   Sales Trend   =   (10 x £1,200) + £83,000   = £95,000

Qtr 3   Sales Trend   =   (11 x £1,200) + £83,000   = £96,200

Qtr 4   Sales Trend   =   (12 x £1,200) + £83,000   = £97,400

Incorporating the seasonal variations gives forecasts:

	Trend	**Seasonal Variations**	**Forecast**
	£	%	£
Qtr 1	93,800	−10%	84,420
Qtr 2	95,000	+80%	171,000
Qtr 3	96,200	+15%	110,630
Qtr 4	97,400	−85%	14,610

(b) Since amounts in money are based on quantity x price, there are two independent factors influencing the forecast. While quantities may be thought to follow past trends in some circumstances, the effect of price inflation will be a major factor in changing prices. Basing a forecast directly upon monetary amounts will tend to build in additional inaccuracy unless inflation continues in the future at the same rate that it has in the past. It may be better to forecast the two elements of quantity and price separately before combining them in a final forecast.

2.5 **(a)**

Day	Shift	Attendances	Trend	Variations
1	Morning	75		
1	Afternoon	50	80	−30
1	Night	115	85	+30
2	Morning	90	90	+0
2	Afternoon	65	95	−30
2	Night	130	100	+30
3	Morning	105	105	+0
3	Afternoon	80	110	−30
3	Night	145		

(b) Day 4: Morning: 110 + (2 x 5) + 0 = 120

Afternoon: 110 + (3 x 5) − 30 = 95

Night: 110 + (4 x 5) + 30 = 160

2.6

Next Year Sales Units	Quarter 1	Quarter 2	Quarter 3	Quarter 4
Trend	222,200	224,422	226,666	228,933
Seasonal Variations	+10%	0	−15%	+5%
Forecast	244,420	224,422	192,666	240,380

2.7

	Year 0 Costs £	Year 1 Changes	Year 1 Costs £	Year 2 Changes	Year 2 Costs £
Heating Oil	43,200	−8%	39,744	−2.5%	38,750
Electricity	61,500	−1%	60,885	+3%	62,712
Factory Rent	80,000	+2%	81,600	+2%	83,232

2.8

	Material E	Material F	Material G	Material H
Current price	£18.00	£20.00	£65.00	£17.25
Current index	100	159	221	880
Forecast index	109	163	218	896
Forecast price	£19.62	£20.50	£64.12	£17.56

CHAPTER 3: FUNCTIONAL BUDGETS

3.1 **(a)** The speed at which the craftsmen work, and their working hours will determine their output. Since they can sell all that they produce their output will be the principal budget factor.

(b) The transport requirements of the turkey supplier will form the principal budget factor. The transport company and the turkey supplier will have a common activity level over the coming year.

(c) The maintenance requirements of the Manchester trams will form the principal budget factor. This will in turn depend upon maintenance schedules for the current fleet, plus that for any additional trams to be acquired.

(d) The demand from the staff at the business park for baked potatoes seems likely to easily outstrip supply, based on the figures given. The capacity of the outlet would therefore form the principal budget factor.

3.2

Period	October	November	December
Sales (units)	20,400	21,600	24,000
Opening inventory	4,080	4,320	
Closing inventory	4,320	4,800	
Production (units)	20,640	22,080	

3.3 The production budget in units for month 5 equals:

Budgeted Sales Units	1,800	units
– Opening Inventory of Finished Goods	(500)	units
+ Closing Inventory of Finished Goods	400	units
Production budget	1,700	units

The raw materials usage budget is based on the raw material required to satisfy the production budget:

Raw Materials Usage   = (1,700 units x 4 kilos per unit)   = 6,800 kilos

The raw material purchases budget for month 5 will equal:

Raw materials usage budget	6,800 kilos
– opening Inventory of raw materials	(1,200) kilos
+ closing Inventory of raw materials	1,500 kilos
Raw materials purchases budget	7,100 kilos

3.4 Direct labour hours needed:

25,430 units x 9 minutes / 60   = 3,815 hours (rounded up)

Basic rate hours available:

22 employees x 160 hours   = 3,520 hours

Overtime hours required:

3,815 hours – 3,520 hours   = 295 hours

3.5 Answer is (b) 600 hours

Working: 72,000 units at 12 per hour = 6,000 hours needed

Basic time 30 staff x 180 hours = 5,400 hours

Overtime hours 6,000 – 5,400 = 600 hours

3.6 Total number of units to be produced: = 27,365 units

Maximum number of units to be made in-house:

(22 employees x (160 + 20) hours) / (9 minutes / 60)   = 26,400 units

Number of units to be sub-contracted:

27,365 – 26,400   = 965 units

3.7 **(a)**

Product	Units	Hours per unit	Hours required
A	240	1.5	360
B	210	2.0	420
C	170	3.0	510
Total hours for department Y			1,290

(b)   1,290 / 300 = 4.3 machines required (round up to 5 machines)

Therefore number of machines to hire is 2.

3.8

	Jan	Feb	Mar	Apr	May	Jun	Total
Units of Zapp							
Sales	5,000	4,000	6,500	5,000	6,500	5,000	32,000
Less opening inventory of Finished Goods	(3,000)	(2,000)	(3,250)	(2,500)	(3,250)	(2,500)	
Add closing inventory of Finished Goods	2,000	3,250	2,500	3,250	2,500	2,500	
Production Budget	4,000	5,250	5,750	5,750	5,750	5,000	31,500

	Jan	Feb	Mar	Apr	May	Jun	Total
Litres of Woo							
Materials Usage – Woo (Production x 2 litres)	8,000	10,500	11,500	11,500	11,500	10,000	63,000
Less opening inv'ry of Woo	(8,000)	(10,500)	(11,500)	(11,500)	(11,500)	(10,000)	
Add closing inventory of Woo	10,500	11,500	11,500	11,500	10,000	10,000	
Materials Purchase – Woo	10,500	11,500	11,500	11,500	10,000	10,000	65,000

	Jan	Feb	Mar	Apr	May	Jun	Total
Litres of Koo							
Materials Usage – Koo (Production x 3 litres)	12,000	15,750	17,250	17,250	17,250	15,000	94,500
Less opening inv'ry of Koo	(16,000)	(15,750)	(17,250)	(17,250)	(17,250)	(15,000)	
Add closing inv'ry of Koo	15,750	17,250	17,250	17,250	15,000	15,000	
Materials Purchase – Koo	11,750	17,250	17,250	17,250	15,000	15,000	93,500

	Jan	Feb	Mar	Apr	May	Jun	Total
Direct Labour (Hours) (Production x 0.5 hour)	2,000	2,625	2,875	2,875	2,875	2,500	15,750

3.9

(a) Production Budget

(b) Raw Materials Purchases Budget

(c) Production Budget

(d) Raw Materials Utilisation Budget

(e) Direct Labour Utilisation Budget

(f) Production Budget (via Sales Budget)

(g) Raw Materials Purchases Budget

3.10

	Month 1	Month 2	Month 3
Required units	144,000	180,000	162,000
Manufactured units	160,000	200,000	180,000

3.11 The amount of completed units that pass the quality control check in May will need to be:

Budgeted Sales (Units)	15,000	
– Opening Inventory of finished goods	(7,500)	(50% May Sales)
+ Closing Inventory of finished goods	10,000	(50% June Sales)
= production of 'good' units	17,500	units

This amount will equal 87.5% of the total production to allow for the rejection of 12.5%. The total production budget for May, must therefore be:

17,500 units x 100 ÷ 87.5 = 20,000 units.

3.12

Period	January	February	March
Sales	61,200	64,800	63,000
Opening inventory	9,180	9,720	
Closing inventory	9,720	9,450	
Good Production	61,740	64,530	
Rejects	2,573	2,689	
Total Production	64,313	67,219	

3.13 (c)   1,875 Kg

Working: Prepared carrots required = 30 x 50 kg = 1,500 kg.
Therefore 1,500 kg represents 80% of unprepared carrots.
Unprepared carrots = 1,500 x 100 ÷ 80 = 1,875 kilos.

3.14 (d)   46,000m

Working: 30,000 x 1.5 x 100/90 = 50,000 metres usage

Purchases: 50,000 – 24,000 + 20,000 = 46,000 metres

CHAPTER 4: MASTER BUDGETS

4.1   Situation   **Contact**

    (a) You want to identify the   Production planning manager
             production capacity of the firm.

    (b) You want to forecast the price of raw materials.   Buyer or purchasing manager

    (c) The draft budget is ready for review.   Budget committee

4.2   Cost   **Budget**

    (a) Production wages   Cost of Production

    (b) Printing recruitment application forms   Personnel

    (c) Advertising   Marketing

    (d) Customer demand survey   Marketing

    (e) Raw materials   Cost of Production

    (f) Spare parts for production machines   Maintenance

    (g) Warehouse extension   Capital Expenditure

    (h) Sales commission paid to staff   Marketing

4.3

| Workings schedules | | | Operating budget | | |

Workings schedules   **Operating budget**

				Units	£
			Sales revenue @ £2.60 each	29,000	75,400
Materials	kg	£			
Opening inventory	2,100	2,000			
Purchases	15,500	27,125	Opening inventory of finished goods	4,000	7,000
Sub-total	17,600	29,125			
Used	16,600	27,375	**Cost of production**	30,000	
Closing inventory	1,000	1,750	Materials		27,375

Closing inventory of materials is to be valued at
budgeted purchase price (£27,125 / 15,500) =
£1.75 per kilo

		Labour		24,000
		Production Overhead		8,625
		Total		60,000

Labour	Hours	£	Closing inventory of finished goods*	5,000	10,000
Basic time @ £12 per hour	2,000	24,000			

*Valued at budgeted production cost per unit

Cost of goods sold
(£7,000 + £60,000 - £10,000) **57,000**

It takes 4 minutes to make each item
30,000 production units takes 30,000 x
4min divided by 60 = 2,000 hours

Gross profit **18,400**

Production Overhead	Hours	£	**Non-Production Overheads**	
Variable @ £2.00 per labour hour	2,000	4,000	Administration	3,000
Fixed		4,625	Marketing	4,000
Total Production Overheads		8,625	Total	7,000

Operating profit **11,400**

4.4   **Materials Budget:**

	Kilos	£
Opening inventory	2,055	2,135
Purchases	10,320	10,836
Sub-total	12,375	12,971
Used in production	10,275	10,766
Closing inventory	2,100	2,205

Labour Budget:

	Hours	£
Basic rate	1,650	19,800
Overtime	63	1,008
Total	1,713	20,808

Overhead Budget:

	£
Variable overhead: 1,713 hours x £3.00	5,139
Fixed overhead	8,497
Total overhead	13,636

Operating Budget

	£	£
Sales revenue (7,000 x £15)		105,000
Cost of goods sold:		
Opening inventory of finished goods (2,000 x £6.50)		13,000
Cost of production (6,850 units):		
Materials	10,766	
Labour	20,808	
Overhead	13,636	
		45,210
Closing inventory of finished goods (1,850 x £6.60)		12,210
Cost of goods sold (7,000 units)		46,000
Gross profit		59,000
Administration	16,500	
Marketing	23,450	
		39,950
Operating profit		19,050

4.5 **Cash Budget**   **May**

                                                  £

Opening cash balance	(480)
Receipts:	
Customer receipts	6,500
Payments:	
For purchases	(2,000)
For wages	(1,040)
For overheads	(1,320)
For capital exp.	0
Total payments	(4,360)
Closing cash balance	1,660

4.6

	£	£
Receipts: (£56,500 + £2,000)		58,500
Payments:		
Materials (£15,500 + £1,200)	16,700	
Wages	19,500	
Expenses (£14,650 + £650)	15,300	
	51,500	
Net cash flow		7,000

4.7

To: Budget Committee
From: Budget Accountant
Subject: Submission of Direct Labour Budget

The attached Direct Labour Budget is submitted for your approval. The budget is based on the following assumptions provided by the Personnel Manager and the Production Manager.

The number of units to be produced will increase from 19,500 to 20,100.

The Basic Labour Rate will increase from £13.00 per hour to £13.50 per hour. The overtime rate will continue to be 1.5 times the basic rate and will therefore increase from £19.50 per hour to £20.25 per hour. The increase is approximately 3.8%.

The number of staff will increase from 15 to 17. The average time taken to produce each unit has been increased from 1.5 hours to 1.53 hours to allow for training the new staff.

The result of the above changes means that the direct labour cost per unit is budgeted to increase by approximately 2.5% from £20.75 to £21.28. This is a lower percentage increase than the labour rates. This should be achieved due to the reduction in the requirement for overtime because there will be a higher number of staff.

The performance against budget can be monitored using the following measures:

- Average time to produce each unit. This is budgeted at 1.53 hours.
- Average hourly rate (incorporating any overtime). This is budgeted at approximately £13.91.

4.8

To: Production Director From: Accounting Technician Date: 23/10/20-5 Direct Labour Budget
Performance indicators There are a range of useful measures to monitor labour cost, efficiency, effectiveness, and employee satisfaction. Staff hours and output data should be available on a daily basis. Labour rates are reviewed periodically. However, employee satisfaction is probably best canvassed once or twice a year. I recommend that we conduct a weekly review of performance based on: Minutes per unit Hours of overtime Percentage of good output (or similar quality measure) Average hourly rate We could also commission a confidential employee satisfaction and involvement questionnaire. A Technician

CHAPTER 5: REVISING BUDGETS

5.1

	Budget for the year	Budget for April
Units sold	24,000	2,000
Units produced	25,000	2,500
	£	£
Sales (at £20 per unit – from annual budget)	480,000	40,000
Costs of Production:		
Materials used (at £6.40 per unit)	160,000	16,000
Labour (2,500 units x 24 minutes at £12 per hour)	120,000	12,000
Variable production overhead		
(at £1.20 per unit – from annual budget)	30,000	3,000
Fixed overhead £1,800 /12	1,800	150
Total Cost of Production	311,800	31,150

5.2

	Budget for the year	Budget for week 9
Units sold	350,000	7,100
Units produced	360,000	7,000
	£	£
Sales	7,000,000	142,000
Costs of Production:		
Materials used	1,944,000	37,800
Labour	1,214,200	23,725
Variable production overhead	1,260,000	24,500
Fixed production overhead	780,000	15,000
Total cost of production	5,198,200	101,025

5.3   170,000 / 20,000 = 8.5, so we must go up to the next step. Therefore, to manage the current output of 170,000 units there must be 9 supervisors, with a maximum output of (9 x 20,000) = 180,000 units.

Budgeted supervision cost must be £360,000 / 9 = £40,000 per supervisor.

(a)   160,000 units requires 8 supervisors, costing £320,000

(b)   175,000 units requires 9 supervisors, costing £360,000

(c)   185,000 units requires 10 supervisors, costing £400,000

5.4

Operating Budget	First Scenario	Alternative Scenario
Selling price per unit	£17.00	£17.34
Sales volume	150,000	144,000
	£	£
Sales revenue	2,550,000	2,496,960
Costs:		
Materials	600,000	576,000
Labour	637,500	612,000
Depreciation	312,000	288,000
Energy	123,600	118,800
Occupancy costs	235,000	244,400
Total costs	1,908,100	1,839,200
Operating profit	641,900	657,760
Increase / (decrease) in profit		15,860

5.5

	Advantages	**Disadvantages**
Overtime:	Known staff abilities	Overtime premium rate
	Good utilisation of own equipment	Staff may not wish to work overtime
	Consistent supervision by regular supervisors	Tiredness causing quality problems
Sub-contracting:	Quality may be contractors' responsibility	Cost (a profit is made by sub-contractor)
	Credit may be available	Process out of organisation's control
	No overheads	

5.6   There is labour available to make **175,000**[(1)] units in normal time. Therefore, **12,500**[(2)] hours of overtime will be needed.

The raw material contract will provide enough material to make **150,000**[(3)] units. Therefore, **100,000**[(4)] kg will have to be purchased on the open market.

Quality control can test **192,000**[(5)] units in the year. It will be necessary to make alternative arrangements for **8,000**[(6)] units.

Workings:

(1)   50 x 1,750 hours = 87,500 hours available

87,500 hours will make 87,500 / 0.5 hours = 175,000 units

(2)   Units made in overtime is 200,000 − 175,000 = 25,000 units

These will take 25,000 x 0.5 hours = 12,500 hours

(3)   300,000 kg / 2 kg per unit = 150,000 units

(4)   Remaining 50,000 units require 50,000 x 2 kg = 100,000 kg

(5)   16,000 units x 12 months = 192,000 units

(6)   200,000 − 192,000 = 8,000 units

5.7   Due to the conditions under which the labour force operates, the labour cost behaves as a variable cost. The material cost is also a variable cost, since it will always vary in proportion to production levels. Note that even though there is no shortage of material, its cost is still used to determine the contribution figures. This gives contributions per unit calculations as follows:

	Bristol	**Cardiff**
	£	£
Selling price per unit	178	150
less variable costs:		
materials	70	60
labour	18	12
contribution per unit	90	78

The amount of labour time used for each product can be calculated by dividing the cost of labour for a unit by the labour hourly rate of £6.00. The direct labour time is then used to calculate the contribution per hour of direct labour (the limiting factor).

	Bristol	**Cardiff**
Labour time per unit	3 hours	2 hours
Contribution per direct labour hour	£90 / 3	£78 / 2
	= £30	= £39
Ranking	2	1

We now use the ranking to produce up to the demand level of first the Cardiff, followed by the Bristol, using up the labour hours until there are none left.

Product	**Ranking**	**Production** (units)	**Labour Hours Required**		
Cardiff	1	2,500	2,500 x 2 hours	=	5,000
Bristol	2	700	700 x 3 hours	=	2,100
					7,100

CHAPTER 6: MONITORING AND CONTROLLING PERFORMANCE WITH BUDGETS

6.1   Monthly Operating Statement

Volume	34,000		
	Flexed Budget	**Actual**	**Variance F/A**
	£	£	£
Revenue	2,720,000	2,856,000	136,000 F
Costs			
Material	476,000	510,000	34,000 A
Labour	612,000	616,250	4,250 A
Distribution	6,800	7,000	200 A
Energy	161,000	164,000	3,000 A
Equipment hire	36,000	35,000	1,000 F
Depreciation	182,000	180,000	2,000 F
Marketing	231,000	235,000	4,000 A
Administration	186,000	189,000	3,000 A
Total	1,890,800	1,936,250	45,450 A
Operating Profit	829,200	919,750	90,550 F

6.2

Original Budget		Flexed Budget	Actual	Variance Fav (Adv)
60,000	Sales volume (units)		57,300	
£		£	£	£
960,000	Sales revenue	916,800	945,250	28,450
	Costs:			
138,000	Materials	131,790	134,950	(3,160)
234,000	Labour	223,470	222,390	1,080
72,000	Distribution	68,760	70,400	(1,640)
85,000	Energy	83,650	82,350	1,300
88,000	Equipment hire	88,000	86,950	1,050
91,400	Depreciation	91,400	92,300	(900)
59,600	Marketing	59,600	65,300	(5,700)
66,500	Administration	66,500	65,250	1,250
834,500	Total costs	813,170	819,890	(6,720)
125,500	Operating profit (loss)	103,630	125,360	21,730

6.3 (a) and **(b)**

> To: Chief Executive
> From: Budget Accountant
> Date: 23/6/20-9
> Subject: Review of Operating Statement
>
> **Reasons for variances**
>
> I have reviewed the results for May 20-9. Profit in the month was £807,200 driven by a 10% selling price improvement over budget and increased sales volume. After flexing the original budget to allow for the increased volume, we are reporting adverse expense variances of £44,000.
>
> The only significant favourable expense variance is labour. This is one cost which you might expect to be adverse because increased workloads tend to create high overtime costs. This was avoided by using temporary workers and cost savings were made.
>
> Material costs were 8% over budget. The increase in brass costs does not adequately explain this variance. We need to investigate whether the use of temporary workers, and the demotivating impact of this on the permanent staff, may have led to higher levels of material wastage. It may be preferable to use our own staff at overtime rates.
>
> Marketing costs were £7,000 over budget, no doubt due to the costs of the advertising campaign, and this seems to be money well spent.

The administration overspend is worrying and needs to be investigated. It could have been a one-off. Alternatively, perhaps there are variable costs such as overtime or bonuses that should not have been budgeted as fixed costs.

Recommendations

Budgets are useful for planning, coordination, authorisation and control. However, this requires the full and enthusiastic involvement of the management team. I suggest that you need to:

- Involve the whole team in the planning process.
- Insist that all known factors and plans (such as the advertising campaign) are built into the budget.
- Assign responsibilities to individuals for all aspects of the budget.
- Allow managers freedom to manage their budgets.

6.4

	Flexed Budget £	Actual £	Variance £
Materials	81,090	82,500	1,410 A
Labour	12,240	12,558	318 A

Material Price Variance:

(7,500 kilos x £10.60) – £82,500   =   £3,000 A

Material Usage Variance:

((5 kilos x 1,530) – 7,500 kilos) x £10.60   =   £1,590 F

        Total material variance   £1,410 A

Labour Rate Variance:

(780 hours x £16.00) – £12,558   =   £ 78 A

Labour Efficiency Variance:

((0.5 hours x 1,530) – 780 hours) x £16.00   =   £240 A

        Total labour variance   £318 A

6.5   **(a)**   **Operating Statement**

	Flexed Budget	Actual	Variances
Units Produced	21,000		
Materials	£63,000	£65,000	£2,000 A
Labour	£37,800	£42,000	£4,200 A

(b) **Sub-variances**

Direct material price variance:

Standard cost of actual	minus	Actual cost of the actual
quantity of material used		quantity of material used
(31,550 metres x £2.00)	–	£65,000

= £1,900 Adverse

Direct material usage variance:

Standard quantity of	minus	Actual quantity of material
material for actual production		used at standard price
at standard price		
(21,000 units x 1.5 metres x £2.00)	–	(31,550 x £2.00)

= £100 Adverse

Direct labour rate variance:

Standard cost of actual	minus	Actual cost of the actual
labour hours used		labour hours used
(2,800 hours x £18.00)	–	£42,000

= £8,400 Favourable

Direct labour efficiency variance:

Standard labour hours for	minus	Actual labour hours
actual production at standard rate		used at standard rate
(21,000 units x 6 minutes		
x £18.00 per hour)	–	(2,800 hours x £18.00)

= £12,600 Adverse

(c) **The following statements are true.**

(b) The adverse material cost variance was mainly caused by high material prices, with higher usage than standard being a contributory factor.

(e) The significant labour cost variance was caused by the labour force working more slowly than standard. This was offset by paying a lower than standard rate per hour.

6.6   The absorption costing report shows that the costs of production were in line with the budget and that the non-production overheads were below budget. However, the sales volume was 200 units below budget, and the level of gross profit was only maintained by the increase in the selling price (which could have caused the reduction in demand). The reasons why the higher net profit does not necessarily reflect performance are:

- The production was not all sold as planned, and the closing inventory value includes £200 of fixed production overhead which is carried forward into December. Continually building up unsold inventory can show higher recorded profit in absorption costing, but is not necessarily a favourable situation.

- The non-production overheads were lower than budget, but this may or may not be a result of management action. It is possible that these are affected by external factors, for example the prices of some bought-in services such as electricity or telephone costs may have been reduced by the providers because of competition in their markets.

The report could be improved by:

- Using marginal costing. This would mean that the fixed production overhead of £1,000 per month would all be charged in November. The emphasis on contribution in marginal costing would show the difference between the original budget and the actual results in terms of total contribution:

- Original budget: £(10 – 5) x 1,000 = £5,000 total contribution

- Actual results: £(11 – 5) x 800 = £4,800 total contribution

- This shows clearly the net effect of the higher selling price but lower sales volume. A marginal costing statement is shown below.

- Using flexible budgeting. This would mean that the actual results for sales of 800 units would be compared with the budget for the same sales volume.

- Giving more information regarding non-production overheads, so that the reason for the reduction can be investigated.

The marginal costing statement would be:

	Budget		Actual	
	£	£	£	£
Sales 1,000 x £10		10,000		
Sales 800 x £11				8,800
Opening inventory	–		–	
Cost of Production	5,000		5,000	
Less: closing inventory	–		1,000	
Cost of sales		5,000		4,000
Contribution		5,000		4,800
Fixed production overheads		1,000		1,000
Non-production overheads		1,750		1,650
Net profit		2,250		2,150

6.7

Email	
To:	General Manager
From:	Accounting Technician
Subject:	Motivating Managers with Budgets

For managers to be motivated by budgets, they must see the budgets as challenging yet achievable. It can also help if they have played a part in creating the budgets and therefore feel some ownership towards them.

In this situation it is unlikely that both managers feel that the budgets are fair. The budgets appear to be imposed on the managers, and it is not clear what information has been used in their preparation.

While the use of fixed budgets is suitable for the pool – because the majority of costs are fixed and do not depend on usage – fixed budgets are less suitable for the café. If flexible budgeting were to be used for the café, based on the activity level of the café itself, then the income and costs could be fairly matched against the flexed budget. It seems likely that at present the Café Manager has no control over the hotel occupancy and therefore cannot control his income or costs.

The introduction of performance related pay based on the current budgeting system would not improve performance. The Pool Manager would probably gain bonuses without making any further effort, and the Café Manager would see the system as unfair since he has little control over his situation as currently judged.

Index

for your notes